THE SEDUCTION OF THE NIGERIAN CHURCH

GARY S. MAXEY
PETER OZODO

The
SEDUCTION
of the
NIGERIAN
CHURCH

ISBN: 9798670367523

First Printing : May 2017

Published by

West Africa Theological Seminary
36 Olukunle Akinola Street
Akinyele/ WATS Bus Stop,
Ipaja, Lagos, Nigeria.
www.watspublications.com
sales@watspublications.com

Contact Addresses:
Gary S. Maxey, Founder, WATS, PMB 003, Ipaja, Lagos
Email: drgarymaxey@gmail.com; Tel: +234-808-726-6310

Designed by **asbot**graphics

INTRODUCTION

Gbile Akanni

When Gary first asked me to write an introduction to this book, *The Seduction of the Nigerian Church*, I had a very difficult matter to deal with in my mind and it made me to check again if I would want to lend my voice to this discussion. I have seen the seduction and deviation creeping into our midst since 1978 and the Lord awakened my heart to stand against it. He showed me how it is coming to sweep away our values and how it will pollute our stream. It came through free books and tapes imported to us from America. It came as several of our brothers began to copy and indeed preach messages of those preachers from abroad verbatim. Our design of ministries changed unto personally owned works. Our method of fund raising changed with superficial and outrageous seed faith theories.

The first approach I had to take is to seek to preserve my own heart and keep myself in the love of God. I knew it would set me on a more narrow path, as I may fall out with several of my colleagues and contemporaries, who were so attracted to this sugarcoated poison. I had great conflicts in reconciling what I read in the word of God, the pattern I see in Christ and the holy examples of the Apostles with the practices of several leaders and preachers. It so bothered me as I looked for men to pattern my life and ministry after and there were very few I could follow, until the Lord spoke so sharply to me, "Have I introduced any man to you, apart from Christ Jesus? This is my beloved Son, in whom I am well pleased, hear Him. Whatever you cannot see in Christ Jesus, you have no reason to follow it. Make sure you build your life, your ministry and all you do according to the pattern I have shown you. Jesus is my pattern for you. And all your valuation and all your estimates must be according to the shekels of the sanctuary. Twenty gerahs make one shekel. My shekel is not that of the world. Weigh all your offerings to me according to the shekel of the sanctuary" (Lev. 27:25).

With this, one issue was settled for me. I will run my race with this single eye on the pattern Servant and I will evaluate my life and my labours in God's vineyard, not with popular shekels or the shekels of the market place but with the shekels of the sanctuary. I will learn only from men and women who mirror Christ clearly to me by their own lives. I have sought to keep at this ever since and I pray to follow this narrow way till I exit from here to His glorious presence.

But the second issue of "What do I do with this vivid pollution and how do I fight it?" was not yet resolved for me. I was so bothered about the imperceptible corruption of sound doctrine and frivolous practices I am beginning to see around the Church, even then when it was still looking far-fetched. My first response was to position myself to preach against it and discourage it. I engaged every ministry platform I was offered to speak on these things. I became, (unknown to myself), such a critique that sees nothing of the grace of God in men other than their misbehaviours. It appeared then as if there is no other message I had to preach. This persisted for a few years, to the extent that it would appear I was leading a rebellion and several people could not separate me from one who always stood against the popular waves. One day, the Lord visited me in a remarkable way and it changed my orientation and it is this that gave me serious thoughts whether I should write this introduction to this book.

I was speaking at a meeting in a local Church in a city. Several people were rushing to attend the meeting as the Lord usually draws men and women to those meetings. I was in a taxi going to the venue myself, when another passenger joined the taxi going to the same meeting. He did not know I was sitting at the back. He began to introduce the meeting to another person in the cab. And what he said was what God used to speak to me.

"Aren't you going for this meeting at the EKAN church? Brother Gbile is in town. Let us go and hear the new release from heaven. I am sure, he is coming with a hammer to crush all those pastors and show us the latest issue. I am rushing there, so I can get a good seat to catch everything"

The Lord struck my heart and said, "Did you hear what men are saying about you? Is that what I called you to do for my Church? Yes, things are going wrong, but it is not criticism that will heal my Church. When will you bend down to labour in love for her restoration? You can gain cheap popularity by pointing at errors of others, but it is a different labour I have called you to do for my people. Do not fall into the mistake of Elijah, who was so overwhelmed with the challenges of my backsliding people that he could not see anything good in them again. I have seven thousand who have not bowed the knee. Go and look for them and train them in discipleship. I will send the rain. There shall be another revival and it will overrun what you see today." This was far back in 1982.

I only pleaded with God to allow me finish the meeting for the weekend, while I ran back to my closet to fall on my face. This changed my approach to this matter. That encounter has left me permanently broken, with the breastplate of intercession on my heart for the body of Christ in Nigeria and in the entire globe. It has opened me up to see the Church from His perspective. Though the issues being raised in this book are real and gripping and it has been the fulcrum of my prayer over the years, the Lord's eyes are upon His Church and the Church in Nigeria will not go down the drains. The charlatans have come; money changers have set up their tables, so to say, in the sanctuary; cheap grace that has no responsibility for personal holiness and victory over sin and self has been preached and aired over the waves, and it seems all will end in death, but what God said to me is: "This sickness is not unto death, but such that the glory of God might be seen."

When Uncle Peter Ozodo came into the co-authorship of this book and that gave me more space to pray, I saw his input bringing some confidence to my heart about the days ahead. He is one I have respected all of my years. His leadership role in the growth of God's work, his burden for the unreached and the many intimate times of fellowship I shared with him as an elder, his wisdom and counsel he freely shares with me and the partnership I shared with CAPRO while he led the work and even now, the numerous times he came to Gboko to stand with us in our little efforts at seeking restoration for the Body of Christ and above all, his passion for the undiluted truth of God's word has made me to lend my little voice to this book, which is a cry in the heart for a heaven-sent revival that will prepare the Church not only in Nigeria but globally for the imminent return of our Lord.

Diagnosing a sickness to trace the causes has become the veritable way of medical practice now and it is cheaper than just swallowing all-purpose drugs. This book seeks such a diagnosis. It may appear as if it is an attack on our beloved Church and the cherished idols of several 'presidents and founders', but this surgical knife is for our good and it is to take away the cancerous cells before they overwhelm the entire body.

I have seen the burden in the heart of our brother Gary Maxey for several years. He loves the Church in Nigeria. He has made a very silent contribution in various ways to her healing. He has sent good books of old puritans to several leaders in years past even before meeting them. He even mobilised the Congress on Christian Ethics in Nigeria several years ago for this same purpose. This is an undying burden in his heart. The West Africa Theological Seminary (WATS) is his invaluable contribution to the redirection of the Nigerian Church to its biblical roots through a theological education that is sound, biblical and evangelical. I have watched him and maintained a fellowship with him over the years. I have sustained a keen interest in the progress of WATS since its early days in Owerri. I have accepted to speak in some of the meetings facilitated by him. He is very open to learn and does learn as much as he can from any of God's vessels.

His submission and relationship to Uncle Peter Ozodo at very crucial times in his life and ministry has made him a man that won my respect over the years. This book is not written by an outsider, though he sometimes feels so because of the colour of his skin. But Gary has incarnated with the Church in Nigeria. He has become one with us in our trials, travails and triumphs.

I am happy to introduce this material to you. It has unburdened what we have severally carried on our hearts for years. May you hear the voice of the Lord as you go through every of its pages. Some may feel sliced and slighted, it is inevitable. A surgery actually wounds but it is not ill motivated. It is to help extract the cancer cells. There may be bleeding, but there is no genuine blessing without it. Fresh tissues are only formed when treating a sore only when the doctors have scrubbed the wound to the point of fresh bleeding.

To the "seven-thousand" company, let me encourage you to rise and press on in the path of righteousness. Some of us have stood this challenge for years and we have refused to bow, so much so that you may have some of us as examples. We have proved the faithfulness of God. His counsels of old are faithfulness and truth. His word is dependable and we have proved it. There is the old path. It is not old fashioned. It is the proven way to glory. Others may berate it to their own peril, but it is the path trod by overcomers and the saints whose life and end we have seen. Come along with us and you will surely arrive safely on the shore of His glory.

In the pursuit of my own cry for revival and restoration, God has used several typologies to illustrate to me what to do and this is my counsel to everyone who seeks the good of the Church either in Nigeria or in the rest of the world. God loves the Church and will not abandon it to form another. Even if some of our brethren feel they are the select or elect group and that God should wipe off everyone else and make them, "the Church," (like the intercession of Moses for Israel at their point of misbehaviour), God will not but consider the intercession of our High Priest, even Jesus the Lord. Here lies my first counsel: pray and intercede for the Church. This sickness that came upon us is not unto death. There shall be a restoration to biblical faith and ministry in the coming days.

I was one of those severally persecuted in the early 1970's and cast out of the denominational churches. We were confronted with the message of "Come out from among them and be ye separate," but God insisted that we wait for what He would do in those Churches ruled then by syncretism and secret cult members. I have seen those Churches embrace the truth and the move of the Spirit. I have seen entire denominational leadership turn to the Lord and Spirit-filled people taking Spirit-led decisions are beginning to emerge in those Churches we called 'Orthodox' then, as if there is anything wrong with biblical orthodoxy.

In the days of Elisha, there was severe famine in Gilgal. Elisha set up a great pot on fire to seethe pottage for sons of the prophets in those days. While the pot was still boiling and he was teaching, one went out into the bush and gathered some wild gourds on his laps and came and sliced it into the seething pot. As the sons of the prophets began to eat from the pot, they found it was poisoned and cried out: "There is death in the pot! There is death in the pot!" Elisha asked them to bring fresh flour and cast it into the pot and there was no more death in the pot (2Kings 4:38-41). Here again is the wisdom He lent me: "Cast in the flour and neutralise the poison in the pot. I will heal the death in the pot. Yes, a wild gourd has been sliced into the great pot and it seemed to have polluted everything, but I will sanctify my people again." The flour is the word of God that must be taught again with all diligence. "Sanctify them by thy truth, thy word is truth". Rather than mourn for the damage, bring the flour and cast it steadily into the pot. The death in the pot will be removed. Let us be diligent at teaching and preaching the word of truth and we will see restoration of God's great pot again.

As you will discover as you read through this book, the seduction came in not through the ordinary members but through the leaders and ministers, who for whatever personal reasons looked for prominence, preeminence, promotion, power, pageantry, and physical prosperity at all costs. The way out will still be through leaders and ministers who have experienced death to self, and death to personal glory and popularity. They are able to sincerely declare, "I am crucified with Christ, nevertheless I live, yet not I but Christ that lives in me". Such men and women must be raised in concerted biblical discipleship and training. They must be exposed to the pattern we have seen in Christ Jesus and the early Apostles. Though it appears as a tedious labour particularly now that men would not endure sound doctrine, it is still our mandate.

Finally, deviation came to us as we moved away from the terms of the great commission given to us by the Lord Himself. "Go ye into all the world and make disciples of all the nations." Nothing else will prepare the Church, the bride of Christ for His appearing unless we return deliberately to build His Church according to the pattern He has shown us in Himself and in the men and women He raised.

I commend this book to you for careful study. Keep your eyes single on the burden behind it. Keep your heart open to its overall objective, which is genuine and biblical revival and restoration. Take note of pits into which others fell, so you can forestall another fall as the Lord may be pleased to move on us again. You are reading this because you have a stake in the coming visitation for which we have prayed and laboured. God bless you.

Peace House,

Gboko, Nigeria.

April, 2017.

PREFACE

Gary S. Maxey

I started laboring over this book more than four years ago. In 2013 and 2014 I hosted a monthly discussion group at West Africa Theological Seminary with animated sessions about where the Nigerian Church seemed to be heading. It was clear that all was not well and that something serious needed to be done about it.

Over the months an increasingly heavier burden weighed on my spirit. After listening for a long time to the writing, teaching and preaching of some of Nigeria's most anointed evangelists and revivalists I knew I could not remain forever silent. What they were saying was disturbing:

> *The Nigerian revival is losing its cutting edge. One obvious reason for this is that there are doctrinal errors in the camp of those pushing the Church forward. A result of this is that the Church is in serious danger of losing sight of the very reason for its existence.*[1]

> *We are still struggling as a Church...The Prince of Persia is blocking our prayers and the prayers of the saints in Nigeria for*

---

[1] Peter Ozodo, "Evangelism and Missions," *Earnestly Contending for the Faith: An Agenda for Responsible Christian Leadership, Second Edition*, Dr. Mayo Abaya, Brother Peter Ozodo, Rev. Joseph Mohammed Ali, eds. (Garki, Abuja: Concerned Ministers' Forum, 1999), p. 118;

Nigeria. I've never seen a nation awash with so many Churches and aglow with so much unrighteousness, corruption and rank hypocrisy. [2]

The Nigerian Church has lost the credibility it once had within the society. The reputation of Church leadership has declined,... we have seen an erosion of our Christian heritage. [3]

Unfortunately, it is now noticeable that a significant segment of the Christian Church in this country is gradually but steadily departing from the basic goals of Christianity...The entire Church is in danger of losing its basic direction. [4]

Many well known Church leaders around the world are seriously proclaiming that we are in the midst of the greatest revival the Church has ever known. Yet nobody who reads the New Testament with an open and sincere mind will agree with those who believe that the Church is experiencing a revival at present...The result is that increasingly, many Christians are living in ways not in keeping with the standards of the Scriptures. Materialism is enthroned and sin is tolerated, while holiness is largely ignored. With the focus being placed largely on the popularity of the preachers, the biblical life-style is largely forgotten. Indeed it is very painful to see churches multiplying everywhere in our country today with no marked change in the ways and lives of the people. [5]

Today these voices are re-echoed by many others. All across the country one can hear disturbing accusations from many who

---

[2] Most Rev. Professor E. M. Uka, former Prelate, Presbyterian Church of Nigeria, email to Gary Maxey, April 18, 2016.

[3] Professor J. A. Ilori, interview with Gary Maxey, 16 September 2008.

[4] Peter Ozodo, "Introduction: The Faith We Contend For," *Op cit,* pp. 5-6.

[5] William Okoye, "Christian Ministry in Nigeria Today: Historical Perspective," *Op cit,* pp. 14, 18.

love God and who love His Church and who are in positions of leadership:

> *Many [pastors] are not called by God but by their bellies... The church cannot help fight corruption in the country because it is itself corrupt...If the river is polluted from the fountain it is flowing from, everyone who drinks it will drink poison...[The pastors] say what the people want to hear, they no longer talk about sin.*[6]

As I listened to these voices I began to see three major factors since the 1970s that are seducing the Nigerian Church. I am convinced that it is urgent for us to have a serious discussion about these agents of seduction. We will also look at a more recent threat to biblical orthodoxy and sound Christian living in Nigeria.

At the root of my burden is an unquenchable desire to see genuine revival all across the nation. It is something I cannot shrug off. I am raising an alarm because of a deep conviction that the Church in Nigeria will never experience genuine biblical revival on any significant scale until we first experience reformation in the areas we describe in this book. The Church has undeniably been robbed of some of its basic foundations and of the purity and power it briefly tasted in the Scripture Union Revival during and immediately after the Nigerian Civil War.

I say it with deep sadness but also with conviction: the Nigerian Church has been seduced. As a result, what it has to offer to the rest of the world is a gospel shaped not exclusively by the scriptures but also by decades of seducing spirits. We are worshiping a golden calf. There is an undeniable surface beauty

---

[6]Tunde Bakare, "Pastors are Turning to Traders," *Sunday Sun* (Lagos), 25 September, 2005, pp. 2,47.

about the Nigerian Church, but there is dire need for not just a spiritual revival but even much more for a scriptural reformation without which genuine revival may never come.

The Church in Africa has come a long way since the days of Byang Kato, the young Nigerian evangelical champion who prior to his untimely death in 1975 published *Theological Pitfalls and Biblical Christianity in Africa*. Kato was the first African general secretary of the Association of Evangelicals of Africa and Madagascar (AEAM, now the Association of Evangelicals of Africa). At a time when many were not adequately aware of what was happening within the African Church, Kato cried out against the subtle threat of theological weakness. He saw dangers of syncretism, universalism, black theology, etc., and with a strong voice pled for a more sound biblical Christianity in Africa. Like a voice in the wilderness, Kato pled for an African expression of Christianity that was nevertheless true to the scriptures and historic Christianity.[7]

I mention Kato because I believe it is unlikely he could have envisioned the threats that we face forty years later. Though he no doubt could have imagined the revival of African Traditional Religion within the Church he likely would have had no inkling about the impact of the unbalanced Prosperity Gospel, and certainly not about the allurement of the hyper grace movement that is sweeping through many sectors of the continent today. Nevertheless, what we need today is another Byang Kato indeed we need several this time tuning in to the contemporary threats to our faithful following of the teachings of scripture, and specifically here in Nigeria.

---

[7] Byang Kato, *Theological Pitfalls and Biblical Christianity in Africa*, Yusufu Turaki, (Nairobi: Evangelical Publishing House, 1975); Jim Plueddeman, "Missionary Impossible", February 13, 2007, http://missionaryimpossible.blogspot.com.ng/2007/02/byang-kato-biblical-christianity-in.html. Accessed 20 January 2017; Yusufu Turaki, "The Theological Legacy of the Reverend Doctor Byang Henry Kato," *Africa Journal of Evangelical Theology*, 20:2, 2001, pp. 142-150.

To be candid, there was a remarkable Byang Kato within the two lids of the Bible. No one in the New Testament spoke more strongly against theological errors than Jude. He was a man who understood well that when the truth of God is under siege it is time to fight for the faith. He understood the gravity of dangers facing the New Testament Church. He could see clearly that false teachers had crept into the church turning God's grace into a license to sin. With the fury of God behind him Jude reminded his readers about how God dealt with Sodom and Gomorrah because of their unbelief. These are the kind of people who are needed today in our beloved Nigeria more than ever. We need people who can truly discern the times and know how to speak out against the schemes of the enemy and unmask the errors and the sin of shallow professing Christians.

In 2016 I released ***Capturing a Lost Vision: Can Nigeria's Greatest Revival Live Again?*** It is an account of the 1960s and 1970s revival in Nigeria. It also raised the question of how we can once again see a similar or even greater revival. This book is a follow-up to that one. The revival of the last generation was the closest the Nigerian Church has come to national spiritual awakening. But the noble vision was eventually lost as the revival declined. My observation is that while there are many good things that have happened in the past forty years the Church has in some fundamental senses veered off track. Yet I am convinced we can and must get back on a sound and scriptural track. This book is an attempt to point out those areas where we have veered off and to provide some suggestions for getting back on track.

Because of my love for Nigeria and for the Nigerian Church this was a difficult book to write. I hope I can be heard as one who deeply loves the Nigerian Church. I have labored here for thirty-five years. I have worked for four years to get my own green passport, as a Nigerian citizen, and surely could have had it long ago if not for the corruption all around us. In the meantime, my immediate family already includes two native-born Africans. I have no home but Nigeria and God willing I hope to live and die on Nigerian soil.

My African son-in-law, Dr. Acha Goris, has helped me better articulate the fact that my perspective in writing this book has both advantages and disadvantages. He referred me to the "Johari window," which is a technique used to help people better understand their relationship with themselves and others. Psychologists Joseph Luft and Harrington Ingham created the Johari window in 1955.[8] Applied to my own situation in writing a book about the seduction of the Nigerian Church, it demonstrates that as a non-African there are certain aspects of African culture and thinking that I will never adequately grasp. That certainly puts me at a disadvantage. Some might even judge that as an outsider I have little of value to say. Yet on the other hand there are areas in which though I am a perpetual outsider I may have the perspective to understand more quickly and readily than Africans what is going on. At the same time, all of us should be reminded that there are certain things that none of us will ever see accurately.

It was because of my obvious disadvantages as a perpetual "outsider" that I was persuaded to turn to my long-time African "twin brother" (we were born barely two weeks apart) to join me as a co-author. I have known Peter Ozodo and have worked with him in numerous settings for more than twenty-five years. We share very much in common but it is quite clear that his

---

[8]Joseph Luft and Harrington Ingham, "The Johari window, a graphic model of interpersonal awareness," *Proceedings of the western training laboratory in group development* (Los Angeles: University of California, 1955).

perceptions of the Nigerian Church are more natural, more accurate and more convincing than my own. It was a happy day when he agreed to jump in and make this a truly joint production. That required him to uproot himself from his labors in the UK as a reverse missionary to the West and to fly to Lagos for long days of uninterrupted concentration.

It is Peter Ozodo who over the past several years has articulated to me more convincingly than any other Nigerian leader an anointed burden for the Nigerian Church. Again and again I have learned from him on these issues. His own spiritual perception and depth was largely forged in the furnace of the Civil War Revival of the 1960s and 1970s. In addition, though he has been out of Nigeria for the past five-plus years, he was at the forefront of the establishment of the Concerned Ministers' Forum in 1996. It is because our hearts beat together on this issue that he agreed to join me in this effort. Thanks, Peter, for coming in as a true co-author.

I must also make it clear that neither Peter nor I have any stones to throw. Though we do mention a good number of names in this book we share generally high regard for men and women in this country who are leading the Church, even though we have deep concerns about threatening error. We speak only from compassionate hearts and with great tears in our eyes and a continual lump in our throats. The Nigerian Church has been woefully seduced. Until we face it fairly and squarely and take the necessary steps to throw ourselves back on a more solid biblical foundation we will have little or no hope for the revival that so many of us cherish and for which we never cease praying.

I am profoundly grateful for the many people who have helped us on this challenging journey. A major impetus came from around thirty church leaders who participated in the Master of

Arts in Christian Leadership module I began leading in 2009 at West Africa Theological Seminary, Lagos, labeled "Aspects of the Contemporary Nigerian Church." As I repeated that course several times I continued to receive invaluable insights from additional scores of leaders from a wide variety of churches across the country. The mandate to produce this book was further augmented by the think-tank I called together in 2013, meeting on a monthly basis, to ask tough questions about where we are as a Church in this country, how we got to where we are, and what is the way out.

We are further indebted to several Nigerian church leaders who were kind enough to read the manuscript and to give their candid feedback. Much of that is reflected in changes in the book and others in blurbs on the back cover and elsewhere. We also owe a debt of gratitude to our beloved brother, Gbile Akanni, for his willingness to write an introduction. Thanks, Gbile. We pray that God will raise up more men like you in this country.

As usual, my support team also includes my wife as my primary physical, moral and spiritual supporter. Without Emma Lou's constant encouragement and steadfast prayers and willingness to give me enormous help with my pastoral responsibilities I would never have the time or energy to write. I am blessed.

My concluding prayer is that God will take whatever is true and good and wholesome in these pages and use it for His greater glory and for the reviving of His Church here in Nigeria.

Lagos, Nigeria

1 May, 2017.

PREFACE

Peter Ozodo

1989 was a very important year for me. I had taken on the mantle of leadership of what was arguably the flagship of Nigerian indigenous nondenominational evangelical missionary societies, Calvary Ministries, CAPRO, the year before. It was at a time when the dawn of a new millennium was beginning to focus the minds of many serious-minded people around the globe on the future. The concern over the implications of the impending millennial cross-over was well illustrated by the popular fear that every computer was going to crash at mid-night of 31 December 1999 because they had not been programmed to extend their dating into the 21st century. Doomsday predictions were becoming rife. It is not surprising therefore that on their part, some Christians were predicting that the new millennium might likely usher in the second coming of Jesus Christ.

Coming into office at such a time made those of us in our mission's leadership determine to plan our work with closure in view. We designed a ten-year plan aimed at reaching the then remaining unreached people groups in Northern Nigeria (at that time estimated at sixty) by the year 2000. We surmised that if the Lord Jesus Christ returned then, we would have something concrete to offer Him. Unfortunately, when my tenure came to an end on December 31, 1996, it was looking unlikely that we would achieve this principal goal by the end of the decade. I became quite concerned and sought to seriously evaluate our efforts to identify the contributing factors to our apparent pending failure.

New Focus

One issue that stood out clearly was the lack of sufficient suitable manpower for the task. We had worked out clear strategies for raising and training the required number of workers to ensure the task's completion. But unfortunately, despite all our efforts, we were able to mobilize less than half of our projected requirement. Suitable manpower was just not available in sufficient numbers. The fervor that had compelled many young people into missions in the late '70s and the early '80s was rapidly waning. Growing numbers were no longer attracted to the sacrificial lifestyle required to leave pursuit of material objectives to chase after the goals of the Kingdom of God.

The reason for this was not far to seek. The message of the fledgling revival had begun to perceptibly change. People were no longer swayed by the promise of blessings to come in the hereafter as the principal rationale for living the Christian life. The soon return of Jesus seemed to have been over anticipated. The new message was that inherent in salvation is the victory we should experience here and now particularly over poverty and disease. Increasingly, the most popular preachers emphasized the fact that we are saved principally to enjoy the goodness and blessings of God here and now while awaiting the blessings of the remote hereafter.

The impact of this message-drift was forcefully brought home to me one day in 2001 when I was preaching at a youth conference in one of the major churches in Warri. I had been speaking on the need for a concerted effort by Christians to sacrificially take the gospel to the remaining unreached people groups around the world. During the question time that followed, one of the young men asked whether people who answered such calls and went to the unreached peoples would prosper as a result. He pointed out that he had asked the question because their "Papa" always taught them to only do things that would cause them to prosper. That young man's question illustrates the extent to which the message of the church had shifted in the country.

However, it must be acknowledged that the focus of the message of the Nigerian Church did not begin to change in the new millennium. The drift started in the late '70s. It had moved from a message that focused on the inheritance of heaven in the hereafter as the major motivation for calling people to Christ. It had now become one whose major emphasis was the material benefits to be gained here and now in this present life.

Faith was presented as the means of achieving this new focus. People were correctly told that God is their Father who loved them and who wanted the very best for them always. They were then assured that He wanted to deliver them from all difficulties and problems and ensure that they have the best of all things always here and now. All that they need to secure this, they were told, is to believe the promises of God.

The effect of this type of teaching was to shift the direction of the prayers of Nigerian Christians away from seeking heaven and the holiness that would make it possible, as a primary goal.

The expectation of the soon return of the Lord Jesus Christ that focused the minds of many between the '60s and the early 80's had been pushed to the background. The emphasis on holiness without which no one would see the Lord became secondary, at best. The drive was now towards what God can do for us here and now. The earlier preachers were openly criticized for majoring so much on heaven that they were of no earthly use. They were portrayed as promoting suffering when God had promised His people enjoyment. Jesus came that we may have abundant life and that life was defined as one of great wealth and unending good health.

NUMERICAL GROWTH

It is not surprising that this shift in emphasis had a very positive effect on Nigerian church growth. The message resonated with many struggling with survival in a society with a progressively weakening economy. Unfortunately, the fact that political leadership, whether in military uniform or in civilian mufti, was often riddled with corruption meant that only a relative few really prospered. The upshot was that many Nigerians languished in poverty in the midst of plenty. Many struggled hard to eke out a living.

When faced with such contradictions, Africans naturally resort to God for deliverance. Therefore, when emerging Christian preachers began to declare that God cares not only for the spiritual well-being of those who come to Him but also for their material well-being, many began to flock to the new form of teaching. The result has been an astronomical growth in numerical strength especially of the neo-Pentecostal churches in the past thirty-plus years.

The neo-Pentecostal wing of the Nigerian Church is its fastest growing and the most influential. In my personal classification, there are four categories of churches that exist in Nigeria today. The first is the Roman Catholic. The second consists of the mainline Protestant churches, including Anglicans, Methodists and Presbyterians, all originating from foreign denominational missions. The third are the mission-founded Evangelicals including Baptists, ECWA and other TEKAN churches. The fourth are the classical Pentecostal churches, also planted by foreign missionaries, and including The Apostolic Church, Assemblies of God, Foursquare Church, etc.

A movement that began within the Anglican Church in the early years of the twentieth century gave rise to the white garment or Aladura churches. It began as an African quest for a God of practical intervention rather than a theoretical God with no meaningful impact on real life. A similar movement occurred among Pentecostal churches in the 1930s giving rise to indigenous Pentecostal churches, the first of which was the Christ Apostolic Church. By the late '60's the fellowship that gave rise to the Church of God Mission had emerged from the Assemblies of God. Others such as the Redeemed Christian Church of God had earlier appeared from within the Aladura movement.

These latter movements constitute what I refer to as the neo-Pentecostal group. They are Pentecostal to the extent that they hold to the major tenets of Pentecostalism including speaking in tongues as the initial evidence of the Baptism in the Holy Spirit. However, they have adopted African cultural expressions that characterized the Aladura movements such as hand clapping and the use of drums and instruments rather than the Western organ as the musical instrument. They also manifested their African character in worship, spiritual exuberance, as well as seeking God to meet practical present needs. It was within this latter movement, the neo-Pentecostals, that the Word of Faith message began to thrive in the early and mid '70s. That was where and when the current rapid church growth in Nigeria began.

Faced with such growth and, in a bid to ensure that it was not at the expense their own membership, many other Nigerian churches adjusted their teachings and practices. At the theological level, they became more accommodating of the preaching of the presence of God here and now for the meeting of personal needs. Indeed, many began to preach the Baptism in the Holy Spirit complete with public speaking in tongues. They Africanized their liturgy and their singing. In a word, they became more neo-Pentecostal. And often it had the expected effect of halting the drift of the young people away from their own membership.

QUANTITY WITHOUT QUALITY

Many around the world have hailed this rapid growth in the Nigerian church as a sign of revival. On the other hand, others have noted how little such growth has impacted the morality of the ordinary Nigerian. While visiting the UK in the early '90s, a gentleman pulled me aside one day when he discovered that I was a Nigerian. He wanted me to help him solve the dilemma of the phenomenon of outrageous corruption and extreme Christian revival as the simultaneous characteristics of the Nigerian society.

I was no doubt piqued by the fact that I was unable to solve his riddle. Yet what probably irked me most was the fact that this growth has not resulted in the increase in the numbers of those volunteering for mission agencies and other services that emphasize the need for the expansion of the Kingdom of God.

Those who join such groups must of necessity understand Christianity as fundamentally sacrificial. While recognizing the blessedness of a relationship with a living, loving, caring God, they see the Christian purpose as transcending temporal blessings. The reason for being a follower of Christ extends to the giving of self and means for the growth of God's Kingdom. A self-centered culture, the type that the neo-Pentecostal message espouses, seems to be fundamentally antithetical to the lifestyle that Jesus modeled and taught.

Therefore, during my 1996 review of this situation, I concluded that what was certainly remarkable numerical growth in church membership in Nigeria did not amount to a revival. Indeed, I resolved that it was rather symptomatic of a church that was in danger of losing its way. A church that was not spiritually transforming the lives of many of its membership into anything that was significantly different from that of their ordinary non-Christiancounterparts was in danger of merely inoculating them with a weakened message of the gospel.

Inoculating healthy people with deactivated disease causing organisms enables their immune system to produce natural resistance to the disease. Such a person ends up not catching the disease. In its spiritual corollary, when people are exposed to one-sided (or partial) truths, they tend to develop resistance to the full impact of the complete truth. As we shall seek to demonstrate in this book, the Nigerian Church has clearly found an effective formula for membership growth. However, by focusing on strategies that merely promote increase in numbers without true transformation, this formula has left the Church in danger of diverting attention from the core reason for its very existence. Indeed, it is being seduced from its fundamental purpose.

This book seeks to outline some important aspects of this seduction. It is a clarion call on the Nigerian Church to return to its purpose. This will not only ensure a recovery of its lost revival but will guarantee it the prophetic role it has been destined to play in the revival of the world-wide Church.

SEDUCTION

The word "seduce" has a two-part Latin root. "Duce" means to lead. "Se" can be translated as away from. Therefore, seduction is the act of leading someone away from something. It is often used in the sense of someone, assumed to be (stronger or more crafty) leading another, (generally perceived as weaker or unwise) into error and destruction by luring them, into actions for the benefit of the former. As used in our title, seduction implies that there is an evil force actively luring the Nigerian Church away from the secure foundations of genuine scriptural prescriptions to its utter detriment.

It is therefore important for us to begin our portrayal with a brief review of the purpose of the Church. By so doing, we can then examine the Nigerian situation to determine the extent to which this Church is being seduced from its God given reason for being. This is not a mere academic exercise. It arises from our recognition of the seriousness of the role the Church is designed to play in God's eternal salvific program.

It is clear from the scriptures that Adam and Eve's sin in the Garden of Eden had calamitous consequences for the universe.

> *For we know that the whole creation groans and labors with birth pangs together until now* (Romans 8:22).

Yet at the very scene of humanity's first sin, God proclaimed His plan for salvaging the entire universe from disaster. That plan has progressed steadily throughout history, climaxing in the sojourn of God's own Son to our planet. Prior to that divine visitation, the nation of Israel had been the primary focal point of the plan God had for saving His creation. However, its role in this programme was completed through the coming of the Son of God. His death and resurrection marked the high point of God's work towards the reclamation of the universe from the clutches of His enemy. When He died on the cross at Golgotha, the work of saving the universe from the destructive destiny brought about by the sinful disobedience of the first humans was accomplished (John 19:30).

All that remained was the dissemination of the news of this great divine accomplishment. It was this task God assigned to the Church as its primary responsibility (Mark 16:15). God's rationale for assigning such an important aspect of his redemptive programme to mere mortals is one that has baffled many over the ages, not least because of humanity's tendency towards frailty. Yet the importance of this assignment is borne out by two scriptures. On the one hand, Paul, points out that this task complements and completes Jesus' suffering on the cross (Colossians 1:24).Commenting on this scripture, Paul M Elliot said.

> *But Paul is saying that those sufferings continue in the servants of Christ, in the body of Christ, as the Church fulfills the Great Commission to go into all the world and preach the Gospel, and to make disciples from among all nations. All the saints down through the centuries are partakers of these sufferings, when we are faithful to our calling to proclaim the Gospel and seek to win men for Christ.* [9]

[9] *http://www.teachingtheword.org/apps/articles/?articleid=73571&blogid=5437 Accessed on 5 April, 2017.*

Without the performance of this task, though Jesus' suffering was completely sufficient for the salvation of the entirety of humanity, no one would have benefitted from it. God inaugurated the Church to execute this sacrificial task of informing the world of the sufferings of Christ.

It is no wonder that the Lord ties its successful completion to the end of time. Since Jesus' death has brought salvation to all, finishing the task of spreading that information leaves nothing waiting to be completed in all aspects of God's plan for the salvation of the world. With the successful execution of that task, the end could very well come.

> *And this gospel of the kingdom will be preached in the whole world as a testimony to all nations, and then the end will come.* (Matthew 24:14)

The Church must therefore accept that the rationale for its very existence is based on this task that we aptly call the Great Commission. The success or failure of the Church can best be measured by the extent to which it carries out this task. Everything else is only tangential at best. Whatever teachings or practices it adopts can only be progressive if it enhances the church's capacity for achieving its primary missional objective.

In this task of disseminating the information of the salvation of humanity, the lifestyle of the news bearers is of high importance. Christians must demonstrate the truth of the transforming power of the gospel through a righteous lifestyle. That is how they can truly be called witnesses for Christ. When we show ourselves as transformed by Christ we demonstrate to the world that the gospel truly works. On the other hand, to fail to demonstrate that transformation in our lives seriously undermines the veracity of our message. In this book, we contend that the type of faith message that has been championed especially by the neo-Pentecostal Church in Nigeria today promotes a lifestyle basically different from that which has been assigned the Church. To enable us succeed in our fundamental task, we must return to preaching the gospel that has the power to truly transform people to Christlikeness. That is the burden of our book.

THE BRILLIANT SUCCESS OF
THE NIGERIAN CHURCH

If it is true that the Nigerian Church has been seduced over the past forty years, it is because she has been standing in a very good place. Seduction implies that there is something good from which one is lured away. One of the most obvious signs of the good position of the Nigerian Church is its amazing growth rate through that period. In short, when we look at the Nigerian Church there is both good and bad news. That is why the first two chapters of this book are about success but also about failure. Both are quite true.

With few exceptions Christian brothers and sisters who visit the Nigerian Church from outside the country for the first time are deeply impressed with what they see. Most of them find it an amazing experience. The excitement of Nigerian worship is unforgettable. The joy displayed by Nigerian believers is unmistakable. The level of commitment to the Church as well as the sheer number of those engaged is amazingly high. Open display of Christian witness is always impressive. Weekly all-night prayer vigils are the norm rather than the exception. The result is that it is not uncommon for first-time visitors to come away with the conviction that the Nigerian Church is in the midst of a dynamic revival.

Much has been written about the amazing success of Christianity in modern Nigeria and its unmatched rise since Nigerian independence in 1960. This Christian growth is all the more impressive because it is against the backdrop of conflict and opposition from Islam, in a country that is split roughly 50/50 between the two religions. In recent years Christian martyrdom has been higher in Nigeria than in any other nation in the world, including in the more widely publicized Middle East religious conflicts. Open Doors USA reported that although Pakistan had more anti-Christian violence than Nigeria in 2016 the killing of Christians in Nigeria increased by 62 percent that year. Yet in spite of the persecution, the Nigerian Church continues to expand.[10]

This growth has continued to accelerate steadily over the past fifty years and now extends to virtually every denominational, ethnic and geographic sector. A leading example is the Church of Nigeria (Anglican Communion). Today it is Nigeria's largest denomination, with a stunning *twenty-five times* as many members as it had in 1960, worshipping in over 10,000 congregations.[11] Just as amazing is the massive growth of evangelicals, especially of the Pentecostal and Charismatic variety. In 1960 evangelicals constituted 5.7% of Nigerian Christians, but today they are well above 30%.[12] Growth at this level is virtually unknown in any other country in the world.

---

[10] Reported in http://www.breitbart.com/national-security/2017/01/13/report-2016-worst-year-yet-christian-persecution. Accessed 21 January 2017. Operation World reports that the growth rate of Christianity and Island both stand at 2.7%. Jason Mandryk, *Operation World, Seventh Edition*, (Colorado Springs: Biblica Publishing, 2010), p. 642.

[11] Jason Mandryk, *Operation World, Seventh Edition*, (Colorado Springs: Biblical Publishing, 2010), p. 643; Barrett, Kurian and Johnson, *World Christian Encyclopedia: A Comparative Survey of Churches and Religions in the Modern World, Second Edition*, (Oxford: Oxford University Press, 2001), p. 553.

[12] Mandryk, *Op cit*, p. 643.

What we are talking about here, of course, has its roots in the modern Christian missionary movement, and most particularly in Protestant missions. It is no exaggeration to say that the single most successful mass movement in modern times has been the Protestant missionary expansion of the past 200 years. Nowhere is that success more evident than in Africa, and nowhere in Africa is it more evident than in Nigeria. In our generation the missionary movement has been both praised and damned by historians, sociologists and anthropologists. On the negative side, Christian missionaries often have been portrayed by scholars, popular writers and movie makers as culturally ignorant, commercially motivated, proselytizing of other religions and generally in league with colonial greed. Yet recent research has shown that such caricatures are generally misleading and often just plain false.

Robert Woodberry has demonstrated, through impressively wide-ranging research, clear linkages between the spread of Protestant missions and the rise of vibrant democracies all throughout Asia and Africa. In Africa the stark contrast between neighbor countries such as Togo and Ghana, or Benin Republic and Nigeria, are vivid demonstrations of what he is saying. On opposite sides of these borders are thriving universities and nearly empty libraries, as well as active democracies and uneducated masses. Woodberry summarizes his research findings in this way:

> *Areas where Protestant missionaries had a significant presence in the past are on average more economically developed today, with comparatively better health, lower infant mortality, lower corruption, greater literacy, higher education attainment*

(especially for women), and more robust membership in non-governmental associations.[13]

Despite this under-appreciated success of the modern Protestant missionary movement, however, it is interesting that the massive church growth we are talking about in Nigeria coincided with the *exit* of the bulk of expatriate Christian missionaries. For the first 100-plus years of Nigerian Christianity, growth was slow. Setbacks were plentiful, cultural blunders were common, and the development of indigenous leadership was sluggish. Political independence from British rule largely coincided with the handing over of church leadership to Nigerians and also with the outbreak of the greatest revival Nigeria has ever known. [14]And then — from the 1960s onward the floodgates of church growth opened wide and all restraints were removed. What followed was stunning.

MISSIONS AND EVANGELISM

What is equally stunning is the growth in evangelism and missions that has taken place through the Nigerian church since the exit of the bulk of foreign missionaries.

The remarkable contemporary reality is the positive impact of the Nigerian Church in other African countries, in Europe, in North America and even in Asia. Amazingly, Nigerians pastor

[13]Andrea Palpant Dilley, "The World the Missionaries Made: The Surprising Discovery About Those Colonialist, Proselytizing Missionaries," *Christianity Today*, January/February 2014, Vol. 58, No. 1, p. 34.

[14]Two accounts of the Civil War Revival (or Charismatic Revival, as others call it) are Matthews Ojo's focus on developments in Western Nigeria, *The End-Time Army: Charismatic Movements in Modern Nigeria* (Trenton, NJ: Africa World Press, 2006), and Richard Burgess' focus on Eastern Nigeria, *Nigeria's Christian Revolution: The Civil War Revival and its Pentecostal Progeny* (1967-2006) (Eugene, OR: Wipf and Stock, 2008). See also Gary Maxey's account of the Civil War Revival in *Capturing a Lost Vision: Can Nigeria's Greatest Revival Live Again?* (Lagos: WATS publications, 2016).

the largest churches in London, in Kenya, in Jamaica, and in Ukraine. Neo-Pentecostal denominations that emerged in the 1970s and that in several cases boast of over 5,000 congregations within Nigeria more often than not have many hundreds of congregations outside the country. The Redeemed Christian Church of God, for example, has more than 25 congregations in and around Atlanta, Georgia, alone. And no one seems surprised to hear that Pastor Adeboye's goal is to plant RCCG congregations within a ten-minute drive of every home on the globe.

The passion for cross-cultural missions is a strong factor in this international expansion. It is true that the expansion of Nigerian denominations into other countries has often been driven by the migration of their Nigerian members outside the country. But the past forty years has also witnessed the birth of a strong cross-cultural missionary burden to penetrate unreached people groups both within Nigeria and progressively all around the continent and beyond. Today the Evangelical Missionary Society (EMS) of the Evangelical Church Winning All (ECWA) boasts a cross-cultural roll of over 1,000 missionaries. Calvary Ministries (aka, CAPRO), founded in 1975 in the heat of the Civil War Revival, is the largest nondenominational missionary-sending agency on the continent, with over 700 deployed and self-funding missionaries all around the continent and into the Middle East, Europe and North America. The Christian Missionary Foundation is yet another cross-cultural mission agency birthed during the Civil War Revival, and there are several others of note. The combined mission forces of Nigeria most of which are part of the Nigeria Evangelical Missions Association (NEMA) represent thousands of Nigerian missionaries reaching out virtually around the world. The former missionary-receiving country has long since become a net missionary-sending country.[15]

A MATURING CHURCH

The success of the Nigerian Church has been far more than growth in numbers and outreach, as impressive as that may be. From decades of dependency on missionary nurture and rule we have witnessed the emergence of a vibrant Nigerian Church that is self-governing, self-propagating, self-financing and to a large degree self-theologizing. It has extended its influence around the globe. It is a mature church that does not take a back seat to any other in the councils of global Christianity.

The organizational and financial structure of the contemporary Nigerian Church is solid and impressive. Much of the reason is that Nigeria has over the past half century developed a stronger focus on education than most other African nations. Starting in the late '40s, tertiary institutions began to emerge in Nigeria. By the '60s there was a surge of public universities in western, eastern and even northern Nigeria. Throughout the '70s, '80s, and '90s literally tens of thousands and eventually hundreds of thousands - of Nigerians flocked overseas for degrees in the world's top universities. One of the results is that as of November 2016 Nigeria was home to 69 private and 82 public universities. [16]One of the clear results is that progressively the Nigerian Church has availed itself of largely bi-vocational leaders who in a growing number of cases are university graduates with impressive managerial and financial skills.

---

[15]Nigeria Evangelical Missions Association lists 82 member missionary organizations on its website. Http://nematoday.org/membership/missions.php?gotopage=members. Accessed 20 January 2017.

[16]*The Guardian*, November 3, 2016, Vol. 33, No. 13,824, pp, 1, 6.

Yet another factor that has aided both numerical growth and the maturing of leadership in Nigeria is the nearly unequaled respect Nigerians have for their religious leaders. Church involvement and loyalty is unusually high. Church attendance is exceptionally strong. For an amazing number of Nigerians their churches command attention and respect virtually seven days a week. There is hardly anywhere else in the world where one can see such massive engagement with crowds of tens of thousands, hundreds of thousands and even at times millions gathering for extended periods of time organized by churches.

Top church leaders in Nigeria are normally held in deep respect and even awe by their followers. They are given the kind of loyalty that was known in North American churches only one hundred fifty or more years ago. Recent research has demonstrated that Nigerian leaders such as those who lead our large churches have a globally unique advantage of being part of a "high power distance society." There is only one other country in the world (Morocco) where religious leaders are accorded with as much respect as they receive in Nigeria. The result is that these church leaders have the capacity to move their followers toward united action along whatever lines they choose. In many cases mere wishes of the leaders become instant commands to be obeyed. Nigerian church leaders have more capacity to influence the masses than any other leaders within the society.[17]

Another sign of the maturing of the Nigerian Church is the rise of several scores of mega-congregations. This has resulted from the rapid urbanization that has taken place over the last forty years. Congregations of 10,000 no longer attract unusual attention. The 55,000-seat Winners Chapel auditorium

[17]James D. Rose, "Leading the Way in Battling Corruption," *Leading an African Renaissance: Opportunities and Challenges* (Springer International Publishing, 2017), pp. 63-74

outside Lagos is filled to capacity several times every Sunday. Tony Blair and Nigerian President Goodluck Jonathan both helicoptered in for the opening of Paul Adefarasin's Rock Cathedral and its state-of-the-art building located in Lekki, Lagos (the largest church building in Nigeria) in 2014. That same year Pastor Enoch Adeboye of the Redeemed Christian Church of God announced plans to erect a three-kilometer square campground and conference facility to accommodate five million-plus attendees. These congregations, buildings and conference sites, needless to say, often display the latest technology and social media tools for reaching especially the younger generation.

Thankfully not everything about the burgeoning Nigerian Church is pointed inwardly. One of the more hopeful signs of the maturing church in Nigeria is a growing focus on holistic ministries reaching out to transform the surrounding environment, especially in the nation's largest cities. Building at least to some degree on the example pioneered by the Nigerian pastor of the third largest church in Europe, Sunday Adelaja, many of the contemporary mega congregations have launched multi-pronged programs to educate the uneducated, feed the poor and hungry, provide medical care for the destitute, renovate and equip run-down government schools, and generally transform neighborhoods all around them. Churches sometimes vie with one another to see which one can make the most positive social impact, and none of it is possible without an impressive amount of organizational and financial focus.[18]

---

[18]Danny McCain, "Addressing Urban Problems Through Kingdom Theology: The 'Apostles in the Market Place' Model in Lagos, Nigeria," in *African Journal of Evangelical Theology*, Nairobi, Volume 32.1, 2013; "From Idahosa to Adeyemi: the Evolving Theology of the Prosperity Gospel in Nigeria" presented at the 42nd Annual Meeting of the Society for Pentecostal Studies, Seattle, Washington on March 22, 2013.

THE INFLUENCE OF PENTECOSTALISM

The Pentecostalization of the Nigerian Church is an inescapable reality of our generation and one that we must not overlook in describing its strength. Fifty years ago barely 1% of Nigerian Christians were Pentecostal. To be precise, three years after Nigerian independence, as revealed in the 1963 national census, the country boasted a total population of 56.6 million people. Christians comprised 34.5%, or approximately 19.2 million. Of these, a mere 1%, or roughly 200,000 Nigerian Christians were Pentecostal, including both mission-founded Pentecostal denominations (The Apostolic Church, Assemblies of God, Apostolic Faith) and scattered emerging indigenous Pentecostal groups.[19] To those who know the demographics that obtain today, however, it is impossible to escape the conclusion that the single most remarkable change in the modern Nigerian Church has been moving from barely 1% Pentecostal to something like 50% Pentecostal or Charismatic today.

Moreover, the Pentecostalization of worship, of theology (at least at the popular level), and of a myriad of other aspects of both corporate and personal life means that it is at times difficult to tell within Nigeria who is avowedly Pentecostal and who is not. Recent studies by the Nigeria Pentecostal and Charismatic Research Centre at the University of Jos, for example, have demonstrated that the percentage of those who say that they speak in tongues is nearly the same among those

---

[19] As cited in Maxey, *Capturing a Lost Vision*, p. 195. David Barrett, et al, *World Christian Encyclopedia: A Comparative Survey of Churches and Religions in the Modern World*, 2nd Edition, Vol 1 (Oxford: Oxford University Press, 2001), p. 549; According to *Operation World*, there were a total of 45,148,007 Nigerians in 1960, of which 30% were Christian, or 13,550,000 (email to Gary Maxey from Chris Maynard, *Operation World* team, received November 10, 2015); Ojo, *The End-Time Army*, p. 16.

who are self-identified Pentecostals and those who are not.[20] As a result, no one is surprised to discover that it is a Pentecostal form of Christianity that is almost always exported from Nigeria to other countries in Africa and beyond.

The Nigerian Church is huge. It is vibrant. It is a joyful Church. By and large it is an optimistic Church. Nigerians love to celebrate, and the Church is in one way or the other at the forefront of most celebrations within Christian communities. Especially throughout southern Nigeria both in the east and in the west rural communities and urban centers are constantly welcoming new Christian congregations, each one adding more color and more joyful decibels to the neighborhood. Christianity is alive and well in Nigeria!

It is clear to us that there is much about the contemporary Nigerian Church that deserves celebration. Despite the rather sobering title of this book, we affirm without hesitation the sound foundations of the Christian demographics in this nation and the fact that the Nigerian Church has the potential to rise to global Christian leadership.

---

[20] Danny McCain, *"The Post-Civil War Revival and its Progency,"* paper present at the West Africa Theological Seminary 25th Anniversary Lectures, Ipaja, Lagos, Nigeria, 18th September 2014, p. 12. He notes, "the Pentecostals are losing some of their most well-known distinctives. In research that we conducted [based at the University of Jos], we were able to determine that only 41 percent of those who were self-proclaimed Pentecostals spoke in tongues. This statistic has been strongly contested by some of our Pentecostal leaders but quietly confirmed by others. What this means is that the most distinctive characteristic of Pentecostalism, the baptism of the Holy Spirit with evidence of speaking in tongues, is slowly being lost in the Pentecostal and Charismatic movements." See also Danny McCain, "Final Report of Research Activities and Findings" from Nigeria Pentecostal and Charismatic Research Centre (University of Jos, Jos, Plateau State, Nigeria) to Pentecostal and Charismatic Research Initiative, Center for Religion and Civic Culture, University of Southern California, 31 October 2012, page 18.

THE SAD FAILURE OF THE NIGERIAN CHURCH

It is a serious thing to charge a national Church with potentially fatal flaws. That is particularly true in a case where there is undeniable evidence of vitality, such as we have described in the previous chapter. If our charges of potentially fatal seduction are true we must be prepared to demonstrate that the positives we have been talking about are outweighed by more sober considerations. There must be convincing evidence that the Church is pursuing trajectories that do not bode well for our future.

In order to better grasp our burden here, let us think for a moment about the fundamental teaching of the scriptures. The primary reason why Jesus left His Church in this world is that it should serve as a witness to the rest of humanity (Acts 1:8). A witness is one who testifies to the veracity of someone else's claims, and in this case we are talking about the claims of Jesus Christ. His claim is that He is the Son of God, that He visited this planet two thousand years ago, was crucified and rose again from the dead for a divine purpose. That purpose is that anyone that believes in Him would be spiritually and eternally transformed (John 1:12; 2 Corinthians 5:17). This change He promises to bring about is fundamental. It is a change for all of mankind from spiritual death to spiritual life, exclusively marking all those that receive Him.

The major difference between these two states of being is outlined in Galatians 5. From verses 19 to 21, Paul states that those not yet transformed are characterized by sin. Then verses 22-23describes those who are transformed as marked by holiness, both in character and action.

John also points out how stark this distinction is. In 1John 3:6 he remarks that no one spiritually transformed persists in a lifestyle characterized by sinfulness. In verse 9 he maintains that anyone whose lifestyle is characterized by sin has neither known nor seen Jesus Christ. Therefore, one can clearly assert that this lifestyle issue is the indispensable evidence of spiritual transformation.

What we are talking about here is one of the most basic teachings of the Bible. To teach any other evidence of spiritual transformation different from or leading fundamentally away from a life marked by holiness is to teach something other than Christianity.

In this book, we maintain that popular teaching in much of the Nigerian Church has fundamentally shifted over the past generation. In many instances it has shifted from teaching the necessity for spiritual transformation characterized by holiness to teaching a form of transformation based on the evidence of health and wealth. We believe such a shift is mortally dangerous. It flies directly in the face of Jesus' insistence in Matthew 6:24 that the pursuit of money as a primary mark of spirituality is mutually exclusive with the quest for God's service. Anyone who makes the pursuit of material things the basis of spiritual life has moved away from sound Bible teaching. A primary search for selfish material prosperity cannot coexist with the drive towards serving God. Making wealth the primary focus of our teaching is fundamentally flawed and ultimately leads people away from God.

Seeking material well-being as a primary pursuit is also inevitably self-centered. It is antithetical to God's call to focus our lives fundamentally away from self and onto God and the welfare of others. Love is the basic ingredient of the properly formed Christian life. Anyone preoccupied with self-focus is fundamentally incapable of truly loving and essentially incapable of being a Bible Christian.

This fundamental shift in the popular teaching and beliefs of the Nigerian Church is largely the reason behind its current failure. The large-scale loss of holy lifestyles among church membership is the most obvious result of this theological flaw. When it became impossible for a preponderance of Nigerian Christians to display Jesus' ability to transform people unto holiness, the Church lost a primary reason for its existence. And it was no wonder that such a Church found itself incapable of positively impacting the rest of the citizenry.

In this book we deliberately paint what may look like a dark picture of the Nigerian Church. This is not because there is no brighter side to it but because if left unchecked, the seduction and error that has overtaken the Church will not only swallow up the light but will be projected to the rest of the world. If the seduction of the Nigerian Church is not clearly identified it will be fatally misinterpreted.

This work is not aimed at criticizing any particular person or group. We are talking about issues broadly shared across the entire spectrum of Nigerian churches. We seek to point out our shared faults as a body. Our hope is that we will encourage those who have not bowed to these dangerous promptings to remain resolute in righteousness. We also hope to help those who have not yet given serious thought to their current beliefs and practices to do so on the basis of scripture. We also believe if those presently convinced of the correctness of what we identify in this book as erroneous will pause long enough to give it dispassionate consideration, our goal will be largely achieved.

Over the past ten years I (Gary) have privately asked many top Church leaders in Nigeria a simple question: Is the Church in Nigeria today better off or worse off than it was twenty to thirty years ago? The virtually unanimous answer has been that these days things are worse rather than better. The obvious question is why these leaders are so unanimous in their response.

The answer is complex. These leaders are certainly aware of the positive numerical and organizational gains the Nigerian Church has experienced in recent decades. They appreciate many of the positive developments and characteristics we pointed out in the last chapter. Yet they are painfully aware that the Church as a whole has been largely powerless to halt the moral decline that has increasingly engulfed the nation, even though Christians now make up a majority of the citizenry. Worse yet, they can see that much of that moral decline is visible within the Church itself. As they see it, the Church no longer has the moral strength or will to lead the nation in paths of righteousness.

The most overriding evidence of Nigerian social and moral decline has been the flood of corruption that has enveloped virtually every sector of Nigerian life over the past forty years. Nigeria has been turned into an international pariah. The corruption is like a flood with no end in sight. Despite occasional efforts at improvement it is sad that Nigeria as a nation has gradually slid into a cesspool of seemingly unstoppable corruption in every sector of the society. Doomsday warnings are not uncommon. We turn a deaf ear to prophecies that the country is on the verge of political and social collapse. And all the while the Church that should be the savor of society is either sound asleep or off on a drunken spree.

Therefore, we must ask, how is all of this possible in a country where Christianity is numerically on a rapid rise and where at least some are declaring that we are in the midst of great revival? How is it possible in one country to have both globally celebrated Christian growth and seeming prosperity and at the same time ever deeper corruption and doomsday warnings? It is a mystery that demands and yet defies easy explanation.

WHAT IS BIBLICAL REVIVAL?

In *Capturing a Lost Vision: Can Nigeria's Greatest Revival Live Again?* Gary observes that the word "revival" has been used to describe a wide range of phenomena in Nigeria and around the world. That has led to conflicting opinions about whether Nigeria is currently experiencing revival or not. Often it refers to nothing more than increased enthusiasm, numerical growth, or widened publicity. However, in this book we are affirming that scriptural revival always begins with agreement with the word of God which ignites a heightened sense of spiritual and moral failure, resulting in deep repentance, turning from sin, total surrender to God and restitution. It results in marked moral transformation leading to radically changed families, churches and communities. Strong movements toward greater evangelism and missions, as well as the addressing of social needs, follow all great revivals.[21]

UNDERSTANDING THE MYSTERY

Christianity is based on faith in Jesus Christ and professes adherence to the Holy Scriptures as contained in the Old and New Testaments. The Bible teaches faith in the finished work of Christ. That in turn leads to a Holy Spirit-induced transformation and to a capacity for upholding high moral and ethical standards. This is true in Christianity much more than in any other religion. To be a Bible Christian is to be ethically and morally upright, without compromise. Therefore, the only reasonable conclusion when looking at this Nigerian mystery is that something has gone tragically wrong within the Church. This is especially true when the Church professes to speak for over one-half of the population in a country that is quite apparently drowning in corruption.

We could come to a wholly different understanding if it were evident that Nigerian corruption is basically a Muslim problem. Yet few, if any, who are familiar with the country share that conclusion. The common understanding is that blame for national moral decline is shared equally by Muslims, animists and Christians. We further believe that since, of the two major religions it is Christianity alone that claims to bestow the power to live sanctified lives, Christianity must bear the larger blame for this national moral failure.

Even more painful is that closer examination demonstrates that the corruption rampant throughout the society is quite present within the Nigerian Church itself. Completely unlike

---

[21]Gary S. Maxey, *Capturing a Lost Vision: Can Nigeria's Greatest Revival Live Again?* (Lagos: WATS Publications, 2016), pp. 243-257.

forty years ago, materialism, title seeking, personal flamboyance of leaders, unrebuked pride, flaunting of sub-standard or fake academic degrees, the "brown envelope" syndrome, etc., are as much alive in the Nigerian Church as within the rest of society.

THREE CONTRIBUTING FACTORS

Why, then, must we talk about the sad failure of the Nigerian Church? At least three factors stand out. The first is that for reasons we will explore in later chapters the Church has been relatively powerless to halt social and moral decline within the nation. As social and economic pressures assailed Nigeria starting during the growing prosperity of the '70s, and increasingly so as the nation descended into economic chaos and decline in the '80s and '90s, the Church did too little to provide adequate moral guidance that was desperately needed to uplift its membership.

In the same manner in which much of the established Nigerian Church sat on the sidelines during the rise and progress of the Civil War Revival, so was it also during Nigeria's social upheavals from the mid-'70s onward. Even the multitude of rising neo-Pentecostal churches failed to adequately provide needed salt and light. Instead, they too often nurtured tendencies toward inward focus that has continued to our own day. By the late '70s neo-Pentecostal churches as a whole were abandoning the gains of the Civil War Revival, especially as they struggled with the rising socio-economic challenges before them. At the same time, they were beginning to import and drink the spiked Kool-Aid of the American Health and Wealth Gospel. It was to prove a fatal move as these newly minted churches sold a precious birthright of revival orientation for a mess of self-focused pottage.

A second factor was that gradually the earlier lines of demarcation between the Church and society became blurred and eventually all but disappeared.

Sunday Bobai Agang, professor of Christian theology, ethics and public policy at ECWA Theological Seminary in Kagoro, Kaduna State, has observed recently:

> *Christians in Nigeria should be afraid of something more dangerous than the Islamization agenda: the ethical and moral decadence eroding Christian public life...I worry more about the serious moral decadence and ethical decline which now characterize Christianity in Nigeria and the African continent at large. Today, many Christians are deeply involved in corruption and flaunt decadent and immoral lifestyles... Christians in Nigeria are dancing on the brink of moral and ethical collapse.*[22]

During the Civil War revival the contrast between those who boldly proclaimed the gospel and the society at large was stark and undeniable. Multiplied thousands of young people making up the vanguard of the revival were singularly focused on "making heaven." Their focus on simplicity and self-denial and on the disdaining of worldly gain was remarkable. Among them there was a visible distaste for the worldly pursuit of money and material possessions. In many cases even such necessities as marriages were postponed so that people could focus on more eternal values.

---

[22]Sunday Bobai Agang, "The Greatest Threat to the Church Isn't Islam – It's Us," *Christianity Today*, April 21, 2017, http://www.christianitytoday.com/ct/2017/may/radical-islam-not-nigerian-churchs-greatest-threat.html. Accessed 30 April 2017.

Nevertheless, as revival fires ebbed there was a gradual introduction of materialism and this-world focus into the Church. The result was a subtle shift of tide accommodating the surrounding culture. The counter-cultural air of the previous revival decade was gradually erased. In the intervening decades the Church has continued to struggle with its responsibility to contribute to the social and political development of the nation on one hand and its responsibility to keep a clear focus on spiritual and eternal values on the other hand. While many praiseworthy gains have been made in the former area it is to be feared that in too many cases the spiritual temperature has subsided and even waxed cold.

Third, it was not long before some of the fundamental emphases of historic Christianity began to be compromised or confused, if not altogether lost. Jesus had declared to His disciples that they were to be salt and light to their generation. Yet progressively within the Nigerian Church the salt lost its saltiness and the light became dim or even altogether extinguished. The result was that the Church gradually lost its ability to challenge the rampant materialism that swept through Nigerian society in the '80s and '90s. The entire nation found itself in a life-and-death struggle for economic survival. Amazingly, though, because of its own seduction, the Church itself was eventually to become the single strongest voice in the society calling for a focus on the accumulation of possessions and wealth.

THE RESULTING CONFUSION

The general picture that emerged during the last two decades of the 20th Century was one of society at large growing more and more confused and the Church in most cases proving unwilling or incapable of showing the way out. Political chaos and disappointment prevailed as in the early '80s the Buhari and Idiagbon attempts at social reform fizzled and failed, followed first by the sudden ambush of Ibrahim Babangida and eventually by growing corruption and virtual tyranny as the country staggered through the Sani Abacha political and social nightmares of the '90s.

In his final book, *There Was A Country: A Personal History of Biafra*, the celebrated Nigerian novelist, Chinua Achebe, made the following assertion about the extent of corruption within Nigeria during this period:

> The World Bank recently released numbers, indicating that about 400 billion dollars has been pilfered from Nigeria's treasury since independence. One needs to stop for a moment to wrap one's mind around that incredible figure. This amount is approximately the Gross Domestic Product of Norway and Sweden. In other words, Nigeria's corrupt ruling class stole the equivalent of the entire economy of a European country in four decades. This theft of national funds is one of the factors essentially making it impossible for Nigeria to succeed. Nigerians alone are not responsible, we all know that these corrupt Nigerians in power have friends abroad, who not only help in moving the billions abroad and help them hide the money, but also shield the perpetrators from prosecution.[23]

This must also be coupled with the fact that throughout this period the Church failed to provide a viable alternative to the

---

[23]Chinua Achebe, *There was a Country: A Personal History of Biafra* (New York: The Penguin Press, 2012), p. 249

African tendency to pin all hopes for economic development and positive social transformation on secular leadership. Meanwhile the nearly inevitable brain drain ran apace as more tens of thousands of Nigeria's best and brightest fled overseas, including many who were desperately needed to turn the tide within the Church. The resulting rising national social confusion was noteworthy especially among the disappointed and disaffected youth.

As we have indicated, all of these matters were made far worse by the fact that the Church was throughout this period either simply asleep, or worse yet caught up in a drunken binge brought on by its own seduction. Gradually the secularism and self-centeredness that had been disdained during the earlier revival were first endured, then pitied, and finally fully embraced.

The gathering symptoms were legion. In place of an earlier focus on self-denial and brokenness was a growing acceptance and even glorification of individual gain at the expense of the group. To a large degree this was encouraged by the triumph of capitalism in the West, where the Church embraced growing materialism and provided a model for the on-looking world. In Africa, looking the other way as leaders flaunted their wealth was first tolerated and eventually expected, embraced and encouraged.

Just as within the society at large where politicians were flaunting wealth far exceeding legitimate sources of income, so likewise did it gradually begin to appear within the Church. As the numbers on church rolls increased, among the clergy financial transparency was often totally missing, leading to a growing number of scenarios where pastors and Church leaders were living far beyond reasonable means.

Scriptures like 2 Peter 2:3 and 1 Timothy 6:3-6 make it easier for us to understand what has happened within our own country.

> *By covetousness they will exploit you with deceptive words; for a long time their judgment has not been idle, and their destruction does not slumber.*

> *If anyone teaches otherwise and does not consent to wholesome words, even the words of our Lord Jesus Christ, and to the doctrine which accords with godliness, he is proud, knowing nothing, but is obsessed with disputes and arguments over words, from which come envy, strife, reviling, evil suspicions, useless wranglings of men of corrupt minds and destitute of the truth, who suppose that godliness is a means of gain. From such withdraw yourself. Now godliness with contentment is great gain.*

These scriptures show clearly how the desire to become rich through religion opens up leaders to seducing spirits, and how as a result they drift into false doctrines. Leaders who succumb to the lure of money and fame become open targets for seducing spirits. This is quickly followed by the desire for a large followership, often driven by the leader's increasing desire for more money. There is certainly nothing wrong per se with large churches, and we can see even within the book of Acts that at Pentecost crowds of 3,000 and 5,000 were recorded. Yet in the context we are describing, a vicious cycle can easily emerge as leaders discover that by introducing new and strange doctrines the crowds increase.

Few will deny that over the years it has gradually become more common to ignore what appears to be obvious corruption, both outside and inside the Church. Eventually virtually all lines of separation between the growing greed and self-centeredness of the culture at large have become the expectation within the Church as well. Seduction is now clearly evident, even if it was not adequately understood or exposed.

THE INEVITABLE IMPACT OF THE SEDUCTION

The eventual toll that all of these changes exact on the life and health of the Nigerian Church has become apparent in two basic arenas – the inner character or spirit of the Church and the outward manifestations that accompany it. So after four decades of seduction how can we describe the inner character of the Church? What are the symptoms?

Though there are many exceptions to the negative picture we are painting, over the past forty years there has been a general loss of spontaneous and joyful spiritual vitality in the Nigerian Church. This is especially apparent when compared to what we saw in the Civil War Revival of the '60s and '70s, which was certainly a biblical revival as we have defined above. In all too many of our congregations we have lost our former understanding of the biblical nature of spirituality. In its place we too often rely on what may be called cheap triumphalism — including rote worship patterns, routine and knee-jerk audience responses, often mindless repetitions and the rampant abuse of speaking in tongues in ways that ignore biblical guidelines.

Far too often the problem of cheap triumphalism has resulted from the misunderstanding of the nature of biblical faith. Reference is often made to the fact that Jesus and His disciples paid much attention to the physical relief of their followers. While this is quite true, it is fatal to therefore hold that the material and physical relief of their followers constituted the primary objective of their faith-based interventions. What can be missed is that Jesus often did miracles on behalf of the outer ring of followers but paid little other attention to them, largely because they would not listen or entertain His demands for discipleship. However, to those in the inner circle, He gave careful instruction to ensure they would meet requirements for entry and glory within His yet-to-appear kingdom.

To distract the Nigerian Church from this latter and more fundamental issue in favor of a primary focus on physical needs is the epitome of seduction. And it is to be feared that our people too often settle for rote worship patterns and routine and knee-jerk audience responses because they have been taught that these are the means of manifestation of the faith necessary for material blessings.

An additional telling sign in the loss of the inner character or spirit of the Church is what can be broadly labeled as worldliness. Worldliness involves taking on more and more of the coloring of the world around us until there is little distinction between those who are a part of the body of Christ and those who are not. Standards of ethical conduct are relaxed.

There has been a very traceable rise of worldliness in the Nigerian Church especially since the waning of the Civil War Revival. First, during much of that revival holiness was taught as the standard and people were firmly instructed to adhere to it. Unfortunately, however, there was insufficient instruction on the means for its experiential realization in personal lives. As a result, many young people quietly struggled with hypocrisy. Second came a strong emphasis on holiness in a manner that tended toward legalism. For example, pictures were circulated showing acceptable trouser lengths for men and skirt lengths for women.

Yet on the contrary, instructions on how to be led by the Holy Spirit through faith into an experience and life of holiness were either sparse or non-existent. In the light of this failure of discipleship, it is not surprising that when the new wave of faith teaching for materialistic ends became the vogue, many quietly abandoned the quest for holiness as impractical and unattainable.

The gradual emergence of an increasingly self-centered quasi-biblical and quasi-ethical Christianity was clearly evident as we moved into the '80s and '90s. The proliferation of titles most visibly modeled and spurred by Benson Idahosa's elevation as the first Pentecostal archbishop in Africa became the order of the day.[24] African culture certainly involves a penchant for title-based hierarchies, yet the opposing Bible teaching of the priesthood of all believers cannot be denied. The resulting unbridled quest for titles within the Nigerian Church was the regrettable outcome. Pride gradually became one of the most unrebuked sins within the Church.

The minimal title of "Rev Dr" became increasingly commonplace for literally thousands, no matter how questionable the ordination or how unmerited or illegitimate the doctorate. Very sub-standard theological schools began to emerge, in too many cases offering "doctorates" in exchange either for money or for a few days of unaccreditable resident study. At the heart was the growing focus on self-centeredness, where virtually everything revolved around self-advancement

---

[24]Before his "elevation, " Idahosa had been quite content with the simple title of Pastor, and in fact was vociferously critical of title seekers. The change toward title seeking within Nigerian Pentecostalism started in part as a protest against mainline churches who, during public functions gave preferential treatment to the clergy hierarchically based on their titles.

and self-governance. In addition, adopting life practices by blindly copying others without seeking to find the biblical bases for actions seduced many from the path of righteousness.

Amidst all of these changes, and particularly in light of a paucity of true biblical instructions, the general lowering of moral and ethical standards within the Church became inevitable. Lack of proper training of pastors and church leaders led to all kinds of syncretism. Eventually fully three-quarters or more of Nigerian pastors, particularly among the newer Pentecostal churches, could not boast of even a solid month of properly accredited training and in many cases training that was available did not have a high moral content. Moreover, lack of accountability for literally tens of thousands of pastors became the norm.

Unfortunately, this also coincided with a historic rebellion from the authority of those who occupied the position of the leadership of the revival. I (Peter) remember clearly occasions in the early '70s where the leadership of the Scripture Union in Ibadan sought to give directives to all those who were associated with it and with the on-going revival. There were instructions meant to control some presumed spiritual excesses, such as speaking in tongues. Those who did not feel that the instructions were Holy Spirit directed responded with rebellion. This began a process where self declared ministerial leaders began to emerge. Though some had studied under the Scripture Union and were only basically opposed to the rigidity of the centralized control of the SU headquarters and its perceived close-mindedness to "spirituality," others who were not adequately trained also began to emerge. All this resulted gradually in a regrettable lack of accountability.

Needless to say, such developments also meant that there was a sharp decline in the earlier focus on scriptural holiness. Holiness as Christlikeness and as a serious lifelong pursuit of purity and godliness became a forgotten theme for most churches. The earlier world-denying focus was replaced first by a world-indifferent and eventually by a world-embracing focus. As the nation sank ever lower into its own cesspool of corruption the Church was not far behind, or in many cases was actually leading the vanguard.

The outward manifestations of these inner changes that took place within the Nigerian Church were many. Peter Ozodo and others describe one of the primary reasons for the decline of the Civil War Revival as the "unmanaged growth" of hundreds and then thousands of new churches.[25] We have talked about the massive and unprecedented growth of the contemporary Nigerian Church as one of its most notable strengths. But Ozodo and others lament the fact that without strong and capable leadership the growth was not properly managed and resulted sometimes in more chaos than solution.

One symptom has been the over-multiplying of denominations. Nigeria has the dubious distinction of being home to more Christian denominations than any other country in the world. No one knows the exact number, but it is certainly in the *tens of thousands*. It would be foolish to argue that proliferation of this type is not a weakness, and especially in view of the fact that in an overwhelming percentage of these churches outside accountability is virtually absent. Moreover, pastors leading a high number of these groups have little or no internal accountability as well. The "pastocracy" that prevails

---

[25]Ogbu Kalu is apparently responsible for coining this description of church leadership largely initiated by Nigerian leaders. See Ogbu Kalu, *The Embattled Gods: Christianization of Igboland, 1841-1991*. (Lagos: Minaj Publications, 1996), p. 279.

in many Nigerian churches is unparalleled anywhere else in the world.[26]

The compromise of the contemporary Nigerian Church pulpit is an obvious parallel of these sad developments. In the earlier revival period there was a primary focus on repentance and the New Birth. Preaching against the sins of the unrepentant was normal. But nowadays repentance is a largely forgotten theme from most Nigerian pulpits. In some cases repentance is defined as mere mental consent, while the validity of godly sorrow referred to by Paul in 2 Corinthians 7:10 is denied. And much less is there talk of total surrender to Christ, of brokenness, and of being set on fire with a passion for evangelism and for holy living. Messages on the Second Coming of Jesus Christ are more often than not part of the forgotten archives rather than live fire from the pulpit.

The strident voice of modern-day prophets against the love of money or the merchandising of the Gospel is now almost totally lost. In its place has come the substitute of a fake emphasis on faith. People are taught to claim promises without regard to biblical conditions. Salvation apart from repentance is now taught in many circles. Just receive Jesus by faith, no matter where one is coming from. Then claim every promise on wealth and health without any reference to conditions.

As if all the above were not enough, the contemporary Nigerian Church has become the scene of seemingly endless infighting and litigation both within and between several church denominations, including some of the largest in the country. Leadership is presented as a promotion to higher

---

[26]Ogbu Kalu is apparently responsible for coining this description of church leadership largely initiated by Nigerian leaders. See Ogbu Kalu, *The Embattled Gods: Christianization of Igboland, 1841-1991.* (Lagos: Minaj Publications, 1996), p. 279.

benefits rather than positions for greater service as the Bible presents it. Churches that once were looked on with respect by others are now held in disdain because of multiple court cases launched by frivolous contentions that in many cases should never have arisen and in most cases should have long since been settled by amicable Christian compromise. At the same time, Nigeria's highest ecumenical body, the Christian Association of Nigeria, finds itself emasculated and caricatured because they often cannot carry on normal business or hold elections without dissention and acrimony. In short, the Church in Nigeria is in many respects not in good health.

PROPHETIC VOICES

The general failure of the Nigerian Church to provide strong light and salt for this generation has been a shared burden on the hearts of a number of Elijahs and Jeremiahs over the past twenty-plus years. One notable example is the Concerned Ministers' Forum, launched in Abuja in November 1996. Activated first as a consultation on the state of the Church in Nigeria, a decision was taken to launch a multi-faceted effort to stem the tide of decline within the Church. Specifically, they pointed out *"the present state of doctrinal imbalances and heretical tendencies in the practice of Christianity in Nigeria today against the scriptural injunction to 'earnestly contend for the faith that was once delivered unto the saints.'"*[27]

In the initial manifesto sent out after the founding meeting, the Concerned Ministers' Forum observed the following aberrations:

[27]Mayo Abaya, Peter Ozodo, Joseph Mohammed Ali, eds., Concerned Ministers' Forum, *Earnestly Contending for the Faith: An Agenda for Responsible Christian Leadership, Second Edition* (Garki, Abuja: Concerned Ministers' Forum, 1999).

- ❖ Lack of sound teaching of the whole counsel of God in the Church, resulting from a poor understanding of Christian theology.

- ❖ Enthronement of man (self-serving gospel) and the subsequent orientation of man existing for self rather than for God, i.e., emphasizing "the God that man uses" mentality rather than "the man God uses."

- ❖ Lack of true Christian values with the concomitant neglect of holiness.

- ❖ Merchandising the gospel of Jesus Christ.

- ❖ Drive (quest) for power and success through occultism, spiritism and metaphysics.

- ❖ Personalization of the Christian ministry.

- ❖ Lack of ministerial integrity and leadership cohesion.

The forum proposed to *"stop this ungodly trend"* and restore biblical sanity by engaging in a number of activities, including the holding of leadership conferences under the general banner of "Earnestly Contending for the Faith," publishing relevant teaching materials relating to the anomalies cited, and organizing strategic leadership consultations for prayer and discussion to foster unity and a proper understanding of spiritual authority.[28]

The Concerned Ministers' Forum highlighted focus on three areas where they believe the problems of the modern Nigerian Church are most glaringly manifested. First is the pseudo-Christian and sometimes outright occult roots of many Christian teachings and practices in the Church. Second is the

---

[28] Quoted by William Okoye, *Op cit*, pp. 19-20.

unscriptural ostentation that surrounds Christian leaders, especially as manifested by the new craze for the office of bishop in today's Church. The third area is the wrong and unbalanced emphasis on material prosperity that overshadows the church throughout the entire nation.[29]

The Concerned Ministers' Forum is not the only example of voices within the Nigerian Church calling for reform. However, the need to bring together those who understand the plight of the Church today has never been stronger. The Nigerian Church is a shining light on a candlestick. It is a city set on a hill. Yet if it is to realize its potential and its mandate to lead global Christianity in the coming generation there is dire need for a deep shaking and reformation.

In the next four chapters we will take a closer look at exactly what has brought about the seduction of the Nigerian Church. How have things gone so significantly off track? Hopefully in the process we can discern the way through to the realization of the full potential of a redeemed, purified and revived witness for the entire world.

---

[29] Ozodo, *Op cit*, pp. 11-12.

Understanding Satanic Schemes

The scriptures clearly teach that spiritual warfare lies at the heart of both individual and national affairs. The result is that there is a great invisible war going on in the universe in which the stakes are high. Satan, our archenemy, is relentlessly out to steal, kill and destroy. He is the foe of any person, family, community or nation that has declared for God. Nigeria is no exception, and unless we see what is happening behind the scenes we may well misunderstand the theme of this book.

The reason we say this is that if we are to rightly understand the seduction of the Nigerian Church we must take into consideration age-old schemes of Satan. We must be prepared to mount an effective counter-offensive against him. Paul told the Corinthians that as believers we are not ignorant of the devices of Satan (2 Corinthians 2:11). Such knowledge and alertness applies to those of us living in Nigeria as much as it does to any other time or place. To put it another way, Satan is an equal opportunity antagonist who seldom misses a chance to thwart the work of God.

There are two factors related to Satan's schemes or devices that may help us to better understand what he is up to with the nation of Nigeria. The first is that Satan is an opportunist and not an innovator. God is the source behind the entire universe, and God alone is creator. Satan is not capable of bringing anything into existence out of nothing, any more than we human beings can. The second factor is that Satan prefers to operate as much as possible behind the scenes without being openly identified. Most of his work is done incognito. Let us look at both of these factors in more detail.

SATAN AS OPPORTUNIST

One of the results of Satan's limitation in not having the power of creation that God alone possesses is that he does much of his dirty work by taking advantage of the weak points in the Christian armor. He is an opportunist, constantly looking for vulnerabilities to exploit. God has made full provision for the survival and triumph of believers. As believer we are overcomers. The full armor of God as described in Ephesians 6 is totally adequate for us to overcome every device of our enemy. Yet Satan constantly seeks to take advantage of any possible weak point and to capitalize on any lack of vigilance.

One point of vulnerability with the Nigerian Church is a relative lack of depth in biblical and theological knowledge. Nigerians as a whole love the scriptures and many years of influence on the part of the Scripture Union has resulted in a strong focus on both personal and family scripture reading. However, there are still major segments of the Church in which pastors typically have never received adequate mentoring or systematic theological and biblical instruction. Some self-taught pastors have done an admirable and adequate job of preparation and ministry. Yet more often than not lack of depth in biblical and theological knowledge has left pastors vulnerable to false teachings, which always combine truth and error in such a way that they can be deceptive to the inadequately equipped believer. Satan loves this kind of situation, where he can jump in as an opportunist to create confusion and sow error.

Pastors and members alike are also vulnerable when there is an over-emphasis on personal spiritual experience and a corresponding downplaying of sound scriptural understanding. Human experience is important, but it can never be taken as the primary determiner of truth. Moreover, our experiences can be deceiving. We can sometimes misinterpret them, but God's word is never in error.

There are several criteria for determining truth, and our human experience is certainly one of them. However, when we place personal experience above sound scripture interpretation, or above the historic consensus of sanctified people of God down through the ages, or even sometime above what is reasonable, we can quickly find ourselves on slippery ground. Satan loves to take advantage of such vulnerability because he is an opportunist and is out to destroy in any way he can.

Satan sometimes also takes advantage of the inborn human desire for protection and for power. He uses it to smuggle in his false thinking and false teaching. For centuries Africans who have felt vulnerable have turned to those who profess to know the spirit world for protection and power. Satan knows how to play on that natural desire in such a way that sorcery is dressed up in a Christian cloak and presented as acceptable and desirable even to believers in Christ. It is a dangerous deception and part of Satan's opportunistic ploys.

One other area of satanic deception that illustrates wily opportunism is that which grows out of the perennial tendency toward Christian legalism. It is regrettable that there has been an incessant tendency down through the ages for believers to turn the message of God's grace into systems of legalism, substituting the slavish following of rules and regulations for the freedom offered by Christ. Paul lamented that even the Jews of the Old Testament turned God's message of grace and freedom into law codes and human works and thereby missed God's plan of salvation for them (Romans 9:31-32). And today within the Nigerian Church there are multitudes who have bought into the idea that their salvation is a matter of keeping themselves within the moral and ethical boundaries spelled out by their church. Whether they realize it or not, they are depending on their own works for salvation, rather than on the free grace offered by God.

Being the opportunist that he is, Satan jumps all over this legalism. He tries to swing the pendulum to the opposite side by peddling a gospel of license to sin. This is precisely the deception that the contemporary Church around the world is facing from the "hyper grace" movement we will discuss in Chapter Seven. Satan has convinced multitudes that all of their past, present and future sins are forgiven and that therefore God is perpetually and unwaveringly happy with them no matter how they live and whether they are walking in obedience to God or not. Once again, Satan scores a victory based on his opportunistic ability to deceive. It should not be surprising to us that the Nigerian Church has fallen prey to this kind of modern (but really not-so-modern) deception.

SATAN'S PREFERRED MODE

A second factor we can point out with respect to the schemes of Satan over the country of Nigeria is that Satan normally prefers to do his evil work undetected. C. S. Lewis has pointed this out in his famous *Screwtape Letters,* where he has also advised that we avoid the extremes of either ignoring the work of Satan on one hand or giving it undue attention on the other. But the truth is that when Satan is openly exposed and is seen for who he is the likelihood is that believers will deliberately launch into warfare against him and will do everything they can to dislodge him or defeat him. However, when he is able to work undetected it is often possible for his damage to continue while believers relax in ignorance and in real or potential defeat.

Our purpose in writing this book is to say with a loud voice that Satan is at work and that there is a strong need for all of us to resist him and bring him to full defeat within the Nigerian Church. He does his work through seduction. He entices us with things that he knows will attract to us. Yet he knows that by focusing on these, we shall lose sight of our true direction. His aim is our ruin as a body.

We are dealing with a common enemy. It is not time for us to be divided amongst ourselves while Satan continues unchallenged. Rather, we must find the means to identify the work that Satan is doing and then to unitedly confront and defeat his tactics.

The unbalanced drive for materialism and the sometimes almost non-stop mantra calling for financial prosperity within our churches is an open sign of the secret and undetected work of Satan. Paul sternly warns us that the love of money is a root of all kinds of evil (1 Timothy 6:10), yet Satan has succeeded in many cases in convincing Nigerian Christians that the love and pursuit of money is a godly virtue. Surely that in and of itself should be a sign to us that Satan is silently at work with his deceptive tactics. He takes advantage of the poverty of the masses to entice them to seek money as some kind of ultimate solution. Our strong advice is that we learn to resist those tendencies as the work of Satan that they really are.

When our people become overly focused on pouring anointing oil on their houses and cars and bodies for protection or prosperity or when they become obsessed with praying prayers of vengeance or destruction against other human beings they are normally unaware that they are treading on dangerous ground which Satan claims as his own. Many, if they knew they were potentially veering close to Satan when they engage in those practices, would recoil in horror. But that is exactly how Satan prefers to work silently and undetected.

NIGERIA IS NOT ALONE

The deceptions of Satan are as old as the Garden of Eden, so it should be quite obvious that Nigeria is not unique with these matters. The details may be a bit different here and there, but Satan's ploys and actions are the product of his wicked conniving over the millennia in every age and in every culture.

A look at what has happened in Europe and North America over the past 200 300 years gives us an idea of the work of Satan in undermining the Christian faith and should give all of us great pause for consideration. It was brave men and women largely from Christian Europe and America who made up most of the early missionary force in what is now Nigeria. They came to us when Christianity was alive and well in their countries. Yet now for several generations Satan has waged a relentless and sadly effective war against European and American Christianity. The Satanic seduction of Christianity in those regions of the world has been enormously effective. The result is that the powerful Samson that they once were has been shorn of his hair and is seemingly headed toward total defeat.

European Christianity was blind-sided by the intellectual revolution that took place during the eighteenth-century Age of Reason and its aftermath. During that period reason was exalted and people began to see themselves wiser than God. Some altogether denied God's existence. Others so influenced philosophical thinking that by the nineteenth century it became fashionable in theological circles to see the Bible as a mere human product and to believe that religion has evolved over the centuries from primitive beliefs in miracles to more reasonable understandings in modern times.

Through that process Satan eventually convinced broad segments of Christian churches that man himself is the measure of all things and that the stories of the Bible were filled with myths not founded in reason or truth. Much of western Christianity today is still drinking from this poison well, and Satan has had a field day as the Church has lost its power in evangelism and missions.

For several generations America was able to resist the tide of unbelief and humanism that inundated Europe. But in our own day America, too, has largely succumbed to the atheistic materialism that was born in Europe and handed down. The seduction of the American Church has progressed these days even to the point where an ugly avalanche of divorce and homosexuality has swept through one denomination after another in the country. The deception is so deep that these practices are not only tolerated but also now are staunchly defended as scripturally acceptable and approved by God.

These successes in satanic deception must stand as a stark warning to the Nigerian Church. Satan is no less intent on deceiving and destroying the Nigerian Church than he has been in bringing the European and American Church to their knees. Paul's warning is timely for us: *"Therefore let him who thinks he stands take heed lest he fall"* (1 Corinthians 10:12).

WHY IS NIGERIA SO CRUCIAL?

We believe there may be even more reason for us to stand against Satan because of the strategic position the Nigerian Church occupies in the bigger picture of global Christianity. Christian demographers have been telling us for at least fifty years that Christianity in Africa is spreading faster and farther than about any other place on the globe.

Gary noted this in a recent book:

> *Today Nigeria occupies a front-row seat in the arena of global Christianity. Our rise to that position has been predicted, heralded and discussed for more than forty years. We are unquestionably on the cutting edge of global Christian growth. As the behemoth of continental population expansion Nigeria is at the forefront of recent projections from the Pew Research Center's Religion & Public Life Project, the Gordon-Conwell Theological Seminary Center for the Study of Global Christianity (CSGC) and the International Bulletin of Missionary Research. They are telling us that by the middle of this century 38% of global Christians will be African.* [30]

---

[30] Gary S. Maxey, *Capturing a Lost Vision: Can Nigeria's Greatest Revival Live Again?* (WATS Publications, Lagos, 2016), p. 12

According to these studies the Christian population on the African continent will more than double over the next thirty years. Clearly, the influence of the Nigerian Church on the rest of global Christianity will grow exponentially. What that means with respect to the topic of this book is that our responsibility to deal decisively with the deceptions of Satan is not simply a Nigerian issue but a global issue. May God help us!

All of this can also be seen not just from a demographic standpoint, but also perhaps even more importantly from a prophetic standpoint. More than thirty years ago Sydney Elton was one of the first people to persistently talk about the strategic and prophetic importance of the black race in general and of Africa and Nigeria in particular. Elton came to Nigeria as an Apostolic Church missionary in 1937, and served the remainder of his years in this country until his death in 1987.

Ayodeji Abodunde tells how Elton in 1984 used the history of the sons of Noah to reveal God's prophetic timeline. Speaking of Shem, Ham and Japheth, Noah's sons, Elton declared:

> *Each of these sons is the head of a complete race of people. Shem became the nation recognized by God as the nation of Israel... God chose them to display His glory and carry His message of deliverance and restoration. We know that they failed. Japheth has now taken up the challenge... Japheth has proceeded to govern the Gentile world until now...Japheth has had charge of the whole purposes of God, particularly in the last two hundred and three hundred years, in the European race in Europe, and later in America. The Gentile world has failed to establish the kingdom of God on earth, so we are seeing the end of the Gentile rule, we are seeing the end of Japhetic rule, and there remains only one son, one head of a new race the sons of Ham. And we*

are seeing some of them come to operation in these last days to bring in, finally, the kingdom of heaven on earth. [31]

Even before 1984 starting in the mid-1970s Elton had begun to talk about a "map of Africa" vision in which he unfolded the spiritual connotations of Africa's map. He noted that the map of Africa is shaped like a gun and that Nigeria was in the position of the trigger. Elton declared,

> *There will be trouble in all the strategic points of the gun because the devil will not want God to use Africa as a weapon to shoot into the camp of the enemy. The horn of Africa is the loading point; the devil will trouble this region to prevent the gun from being loaded. The outlet of the bullet South Africa, is bound by apartheid to prevent the bullet from being discharged, but the outlet will be opened. Nigeria occupies the position of the trigger, and the devil will do all he can [even if the gun is loaded] to stop the trigger from being released. [32]*

No matter how significant or accurate this spiritualizing of the African map may be, our point here is that there can be no doubt that Nigeria as the behemoth of the continent is highly strategic not just for itself but for the entire continent and beyond to the entirety of global Christianity. We must win the battle that is before us! And if there ever was a time in our history when it was absolutely paramount to understand the deceptions of Satan it is today.

The good news is that God has given us every necessary tool to achieve victory as a nation. If we can arise unitedly to confront

---

[31]Ayodeji Abodunde, *A Heritage of Faith: A History of Christianity in Nigeria* (Ibadan: PierceWatershed, 2009), p. 345. For a comprehensive study of Elton's life and his impact on Nigerian Pentecostalism see Ayodeji Abodunde, *Messenger: Sydney Elton and the Making of Pentecostalism in Nigeria* (Lagos: PierceWatershed, 2016).
[32]Abodunde, *Heritage*, p. 346.

the seduction that surrounds us it will have implications that will go far beyond our own borders and extend far beyond our own generation. This is our firm belief. Satan is a formidable foe, but he can and must be totally defeated.

THE DEADLY ALLURE OF PROSPERITY

The seduction of the Nigerian Church is neither a simple matter nor something that happened over a short period of time. There have been many contributing factors and the seduction has gone on for most of the past fifty years. Tracing adequately all of the sources of this problem would take more space than could be managed in a single volume. Therefore, we will describe in this book what we believe are the three most evident sources of the seduction of the Nigerian Church. In this chapter we will explore the fatal attraction of the American Health and Wealth Gospel, exposing how it has seduced the Nigerian Church and where it deviates from the plain truth of the Scriptures. In the following chapter we will look at the mounting revival of African Traditional Religion within the Church, both in its overt and covert manifestations, and how that, too, has pulled us away from the foundations of the Holy Bible. In Chapter Six we will examine the less well understood subtle but lethal redefinition of Christian spirituality that has helped drive major segments of the Church off its foundations.

Before we launch into an analysis of these issues, however, we believe it is important to remind our readers that we are not talking about a problem of Church teachers or leaders with sinister motives. No doubt the Church of Jesus Christ has always had at least a small degree of such people, but we firmly believe the Nigerian Church has been blessed with a high number of dedicated, sincere and righteous leaders. The writer to the Hebrews describes what we are talking about:

> *Furthermore, we have had human fathers who corrected us, and we paid them respect. Shall we not much more readily be in subjection to the Father of spirits and live? For they indeed for a few days chastened us as seemed best to them, but He for our profit, that we may be partakers of His holiness.* (Hebrews 12:9-10)

We, too, owe a lot of respect to our Nigerian church leaders who have labored over the decades to do what is right and to teach what is right and to guide God's people faithfully. And we can wholeheartedly say that even though errors may have been made along the way, including sometimes errors with very grave consequences, these people truly did what "seemed best to them." We deliberately honor them for all they achieved for the glory of God.

HOW HAS SO MUCH CHANGED?

It is not possible to paint with a single brush stroke a description of the Nigerian Church. It is a very multi-faceted phenomenon. Therefore, what we are writing about in this book is true of the Nigerian Church in varying degrees. However, at the risk of over-generalization, we maintain that the basic character of much of the Nigerian Church has profoundly changed during the present generation. If an outside visitor could drop into Nigeria in 1975 and visit a cross-section of ten churches and later drop into Nigeria in 2017 and visit a similar cross-section of ten churches there would be many similarities but also profound differences. There have been undeniable major changes in the Nigerian Church, but what are they?

Aside from the substantial numerical growth of the Nigerian Church, the most visible difference is the decisive Pentecostalization all over the nation. As pointed out in Chapter One, this has to do primarily with the numerical triumph of Pentecostal and Charismatic congregations in Nigeria. Hardly anywhere else in the world have we seen such a rapid rise from less than 1% of all Nigerian Christians fifty years ago to somewhere around 50% today. It is our belief that the result has been generally of great blessing to the entire nation.

Even beyond rapidly rising numbers of those who call themselves Pentecostal is the fact that Pentecostalism has impacted Christian worship and theology in virtually *all* denominations in Nigeria. Even in our most liturgical churches including the Roman Catholic Church singing and clapping of hands common in Pentecostal churches, borrowing of Pentecostal-originated choruses, and preaching on Pentecostal-inspired themes has become almost universal. The fact that nearly one-half of Nigerian Christians who do not label themselves Pentecostal speak in tongues is yet another sign of the pervasive impact of Pentecostalism.[33]

However, what we are focusing on in this chapter goes far deeper than worship styles and speaking in tongues. For much of the Nigerian Church the basic understanding of church and

---

[33] Danny McCain, "Final Report of Research Activities and Findings" from Nigeria Pentecostal and Charismatic Research Centre (University of Jos, Jos, Plateau State, Nigeria) to Pentecostal and Charismatic Research Initiative, Center for Religion and Civic Culture, University of Southern California, 31 October 2012, page 18.

worship and religion in general has subtly shifted from unmistakable God-centeredness to a disturbing self-centeredness. In today's Nigeria, church is for many people not where one goes to give or to surrender or to prostrate, but rather where one goes to get, to decree and even to demand.[34] The focus has shifted from surrender to God to the cajoling or manipulating of God for the fulfillment of personal desires. Faith as simple trust in a Heavenly Father has turned into inappropriate demandingness, where faith is seen as a tool for obtaining material gain. The primary aim is no longer spiritual transformation and preparation for a holy heaven but rather strategic positioning for earthly comfort. In short, the Nigerian Church has become worldly-minded and earth-centered. We have not adequately pondered Jesus' piercing question, *"What will a man give in exchange for his soul?"* (Matthew 16:26). Sadly, it reminds us of the time in the desert during the exodus when Israel worshiped the golden calf.

We are saying that a major characteristic of the contemporary Nigerian Church in which it differs markedly from its 1975 antecedents is the pronounced focus on *material prosperity*. Material prosperity is certainly an important focus, and especially for Nigerians who have progressively found themselves at wits end to know how to physically survive. But the pendulum has swung too far in the wrong direction. In much of the contemporary Nigerian Church, hunger for a holy God has been largely replaced by hunger for material prosperity. Dedication to God has been replaced by dedication

---

[34]Tokunboh Adeyemo laments that "the African peoples do not seek God for His own sake. They seek Him in worship for what they can get out of Him. Mbiti has rightly described their objective as utilitarian [practical]. It is a means to exploit [use for one's advantage] rather than veneration [worship]" *Salvation in African Tradition*. Nairobi: Evangel Publishing House, 1979, p. 47, quoted by Richard Gehman, *African Traditional Religion in the Light of the Bible* (Jos: Africa Christian Textbooks, First edition, 2001; 2013), p. 246.

to financial success. As the emphasis has continued doors have been opened to bring in unethical, corrupt and worldly elements, all in the name of prosperity.

How did this happen? What brought about such profound changes? How could the foundations of our understanding have so radically shifted in a single generation? Most of the answer goes back to the '70s. If we trace it properly we discover the influence of unbalanced teachings and practices imported from the questionable fringes of American Pentecostalism. If we then add the growing attraction of impoverished Nigerians to the increasingly lavish lifestyles of Americans we can better understand what has happened. Even while Nigerians were dying under the crushing financial woes of the '80s and '90s, the glitter of American wealth was progressively brought into Nigerian Christian homes via media such as CNN. Even more telling, however, was Trinity Broadcasting Network (TBN). Pentecostal and charismatic TV programming in Africa rose to over 150 million homes by the first decade of the new century, and it was overwhelmingly influenced by purveyors of the Health and Wealth Gospel. It has proved an irresistible attraction.[35]

At an earlier stage in the '30s British Pentecostals introduced Nigeria to international Pentecostalism, with the rise of the Apostolic Church, which remains today the largest Nigerian Pentecostal denomination. By the '40s the American Assemblies of God Church arrived. The American Foursquare Gospel Church came in the '50s. Today these Pentecostal groups count Nigerian congregations in the

---

[35]Isaac Phiri and Joe Maxwell, "Gospel Riches: Africa's rapid embrace of prosperity Pentecostalism provokes concern and hope," *Christianity Today*, July 2007, Vol. 57, No. 7, p. 23.

thousands, and the first two count membership in the millions.

These international Pentecostal groups are part of classical or mainstream Pentecostalism, directly tracing lineage to the great 1906 Azusa Street birth of global Pentecostalism. But importantly, all three of these groups at various points deliberately distanced themselves from the teaching of the American Health and Wealth movement. They issued proclamations denouncing false teachings that sadly were to eventually seduce much of Nigerian Pentecostalism and today still reign unchecked in many of our churches.[36] Their most revered teachers and scholars have warned against the theological errors.[37] Even today the Word of Faith theology, though normally proclaimed by sincere and godly leaders, is understood by much of mainstream Pentecostalism as unfaithful to orthodox or biblical Christian teaching.[38]

Others have told the story of how this theological and scriptural flawed teaching was introduced to Nigerian Pentecostalism and eventually seduced wide swaths of the

---

[36]The Assemblies of God, for example, in an official denominational statement, stated that behind the Word of Faith attempt to "use God's ability and power" is a mindset in which man is in charge rather than God. "This puts man in the position of using God, rather than man surrendering himself to be used of God." *The Believer and Positive Confession* (Springfield, MO: Gospel Publishing House, 1980), p. 17.

[37]See, e.g., Oral Roberts University professor Charles Farah, Jr., *From the Pinnacle of the Temple: Faith vs. Presumption* (Plainfield, NJ, 1979); Assemblies of God scholar Gordon Fee, "The Disease of the Health and Wealth Gospels," (Costa Mesa: Word for Today, 1979); D. R. McConnell, *A Different Gospel* (Peabody, MA: Hendrickson, 1988).

[38]It is interesting to observe that the recent election of Donald J. Trump as US president has served to nudge the prosperity message a bit more into the American consciousness and Christian mainstream. In view of its serious core errors we find this disconcerting. Over a two-year period Paula White, who shamefully divorced her fellow pastor/husband of many years in 2007, has formed a close relationship with Trump, in part because of the prosperity teaching mantra that wealth is a sign of God's blessing, even though Trump has apparently not shown over the years any consistent evidence of biblical conversion and has at times exhibited a lifestyle contrary to scriptural morality. Paula White was among

Nigerian Church.[39] Here we can only trace broad outlines. To get the whole story we would have to discuss in detail the contributions of E. W. Kenyon, John G. Lake, Gordon Lindsay, Benson Idahosa, Kenneth Hagin, T. L. Osborn, Fred Price and several others. Along the way we would hear strange teachings about Jesus becoming God at His baptism, about Jesus dying spiritually as well as physically, about sense knowledge and revelation knowledge, and about human beings in "God's class" and therefore being gods themselves.

A significant part of the background for the introduction of Word of Faith teaching into Nigeria was the distribution of the writings of E. W. Kenyon, starting in the 1950s. I (Gary) had never heard of E. W. Kenyon before my arrival in Nigeria in 1982, but I quickly discovered his dog-eared and well-marked books on the shelves of my first Nigerian mentor.[40] I was later to discover that my mentor was only one of thousands of Nigerian pastors who were eagerly devouring Kenyon's books.

Essek William Kenyon (1867-1948) is regarded by many as the originator of "positive confession" teaching, though there is controversy among his biographers about what influences he drew from in developing his theology.[41] He was a holiness

---

the six clergy invited to offer prayers at Trump's inauguration in January 2017. We must remember that the prosperity message should be judged by its faithfulness to the Bible and not by those it attracts. Kate Shellnutt, "The Story Behind Trump's Controversial Prayer Partner: What Paula White's Washington Moment Implies For the Prosperity Gospel's Future," *Christianity Today*, January 19, 2017, http://www.christianitytoday.com/ct/2017/january-web-only/paula-white-donald-trump-prayer-partner-inauguration.html. Accessed 21 January 2017.

[39] Ayodeji Abodunde, *A Heritage of Faith: A History of Christianity in Nigeria* (Ibadan: Pierce Watershed, 2009), pp. 592-598.

[40] Gary S. Maxey, *The WATS Journey: A Personal Narrative* (Lagos, WATS Publications, 2014), pp. 44-45, 50-51.

[41] Researchers D. R. McConnell and Charles Farah, Jr. assert that Kenyon was directly or indirectly influenced by the nineteenth-century metaphysical cults that produced Christian Science, while Joe McIntyre makes the counter-claim that Kenyon's teachings

evangelist, pastor, educator and author of sixteen books. Although he was not a Pentecostal he nevertheless is understood as the grandfather of the Word of Faith movement.

Kenyon's positive confession teaching was accepted and then popularized by the undisputed father of the Word of Faith movement, Kenneth E. Hagin. Kenyon's teaching was that we can literally bring into existence what we state with our mouths, because faith is a confession, and words have great power. In short, believers can get rich by mustering enough faith and saying the right words. *"Say it, do it, receive it, tell it,"* was Hagin's simple message. The power of the tongue in positive confession became a major theme for men such as Kenneth Hagin (often talking about faith as a "force" that produces material wealth), Kenneth Copeland, Charles Capps, and a host of others, including contemporary teachers such as Benny Hinn, Joel Osteen and Joseph Prince.

As we will see more clearly below when we look at the scriptural teaching about prosperity, the Word of Faith movement was not totally wrong about what they were teaching. Their error is that they present a dangerously unbalanced perspective. The scriptural teaching that *"life and death are in the power of the tongue"* (Proverbs 18:21) is that our words potentially either build us up or tear us down. The description of young David's encounter with Goliath as recorded in 1 Samuel 17 is a remarkable example of the importance of speaking the will of God with confident assurance (especially verses 45-47), followed by total victory.

---

were more clearly based on champions of the American holiness movement such as A. J. Gordon, A. T. Pierson and A. B. Simpson. See D. R. McConnell, *A Different Gospel, Updated Edition* (Peabody, MA: Hendrickson Publishers, 1988, 1995); Charles Farah, Jr., *From the Pinnacle of the Temple: Faith vs. Presumption* (Plainfield, NJ: Logos International, 1979); Joe McIntyre, *E. W. Kenyon and His Message of Faith: The True Story* (Bothell, WA: Empowering Grace Ministries, 1997).

Jesus Himself, as we can see in John 5, was careful to note, *"the Son can do nothing of Himself"* (v. 19). Moreover, Jesus said, *"I can of Myself do nothing. . . because I do not seek My own will but the will of the Father who sent Me"* (v. 30).Both in the case of David and Jesus, we can certainly see that words are important. But we can also see that our words must be both inspired by the Spirit of God (i.e., in total harmony with the will of God), and also such that truly build the kingdom of heaven. However, to go beyond that, as the Word of Faith teachers have often done, and to turn words into a "force" that can be operated even for personal purposes and that can be equated to God's creative powers is going much too far.

After Kenyon's death in 1948 his daughter launched a strong effort to disseminate his books throughout sub-Sahara Africa, and especially within Nigeria. Of even greater significance, however, was the fact that Kenyon's books were picked up, devoured, and widely amplified by a young, energetic and godly Pentecostal pastor in Tulsa, Oklahoma, Kenneth Hagin. He it was who became the guiding star behind the Word of Faith Movement, amplifying Kenyon's teachings a hundredfold, even to the extent of publishing several volumes of his own drawn often word-for-word from Kenyon.[42]

The impact of these developments on Nigerian neo-Pentecostalism, however, required mediating influences. Those influences soon became available through the efforts of Sydney Elton and Benson Idahosa. Though he lived to regret some of the consequences, Elton was one of the earliest and strongest links between American and Nigerian

---

[42]D. R. McConnell clearly demonstrates Hagin's plagiarism in *A Different Gospel*, pp. 6-11.

Pentecostalism.[43] That he regretted it was quite apparently due to the fact that his linkages were not as much with mainstream North American Pentecostalism as with fringe Pentecostal movements such as the Word of Faith and Latter Rain movements.[44]

Elton also was the person who introduced the young Benson Idahosa to Gordon Lindsay of the Christ for All Nations Institute in Dallas, Texas. Lindsay had his own earlier connections with Pentecostals and healers such as Alexander Dowie and John G. Lake. Starting with his exposure to Gordon Lindsay, Benson Idahosa quickly overtook Elton as Nigeria's strongest linkage with American Pentecostalism. He made literally hundreds of visits to Pentecostal destinations in North America between the late '70s and his regrettable sudden death in 1998.

The capstone in the capitulation of Nigerian Pentecostalism to the Word of Faith movement came in the mid-'70s and beyond, as more and more Nigerian neo-Pentecostal attention became riveted on Kenneth Hagin. Hagin's books and tapes

---

[43] Ayodeji Abodunde describes Elton's role at length in *Messenger: Sydney Elton and the Making of Pentecostalism in Nigeria* (Lagos: PierceWatershed, 2016), including evidences of his regrets especially in the last five years of his life (e.g., pp. 310-320).

[44] The Latter Rain Movement was a controversial movement within Canadian and American Pentecostalism that arose in the late '40s and '50s and eventually spread to other countries. It was influenced by the questionable teachings of William Branham and Franklin Hall and also emphasized such relatively new things as the laying on of hands (in contrast to the older Pentecostal practice of "tarrying" for the Holy Spirit), extra-biblical revelation (personal prophecies, and directives straight from God), the restoration of the offices of prophet and apostle, deliverance ministries and encouraging more energetic Spirit-focused praise and worship. Hundreds of nondenominational churches emerged in the wake of this movement. Eventually several of these practices became accepted as mainstream within Pentecostalism, including in Nigeria. For several years Sydney Elton promoted the Latter Rain Movement in Nigeria. Yet the Assemblies of God and the Apostolic Church officially rejected the more radical teachings of the movement. See R. M. Riss, "Latter Rain Movement," *Dictionary of Pentecostal and Charismatic Movements*, Stanley M. Burgess and Gary B. McGee, eds. (Grand Rapids: Zondervan Publishing House, 1988), pp. 532-534.

flooded the Nigerian religious market in the millions. Starting in 1978, Hagin's annual camp meetings became a veritable Mecca for a growing number of leaders within Nigerian neo-Pentecostalism. All roads now led to Tulsa, Oklahoma.[45]

Our point is that this was not simply fascination with American Pentecostalism but rather a fixation on relatively unbalanced teachings that came not from the mainstream of American Pentecostalism but from its fringe. Certainly tens of thousands of American Pentecostals embraced such teaching, but they were far outnumbered by those who did not. No one doubted the sincerity and warmth and spiritual vitality of Kenneth Hagin, and even more so as he advanced in years. Yet his teaching had launched a whole new theological thrust that was to have widening impact and truly global consequences. Later Nigeria visits by T. L. Osborn, Morris Cerullo and Fred Price only served to further cement the fascination of much of Nigerian Pentecostalism with Word of Faith teaching augmented by the distribution of millions of books, tapes and pamphlets heralding this new theology.

---

[45]Gary S. Maxey, *Capturing a Lost Vision: Can Nigeria's Greatest Revival Live Again?* (Lagos: WATS Publications, 2016), pp. 233-235; while Hagin eventually virtually mesmerized thousands of Nigerian pastors, none may have been more enamored than David Oyedepo. According to his testimony, *"Having been a student of Kenneth E. Hagin for over 20 years, and excitedly following his ministry through his books, one day the Lord showed me a picture of Hagin while in my study room at about 5 a.m. and said to me, "Look at this man," and I looked up. He then went on to say, "Pattern your ministry after this man." . . . I craved the unction upon Hagin so badly that when I was at his meeting in 1986, I said, "Lord, whatever makes Hagin Hagin, I want it. I want his serenity, the calmness of his ministry and the noiselessness of his effect." I knew that one didn't have to make noise to make news. Hagin was sitting in a little corner from where he was turning the entire world around by the Spirit of God. So I said to God, "I desire this." As I was looking at him ministering from the gallery where I sat, the power of God fell on me! I broke down in tears, weeping profusely and uncontrollably, and the Lord said, "My son, David, the baton has been passed over to you." . . . The truth is that where Hagin stopped is where the second faith movement is starting, and our ministry is not just a ministry, but a movement. . . . Hagin led a faith movement in the first order, and God has given me the baton to lead the faith movement for the second order. I believe in Kenneth E. Hagin, I believe in his God and in what he carried."* David O. Oyedepo, *Exploits in Ministry*, 2006, reprinted 2013, Dominion Press, pp. 269-270.

There were other factors that ensured the domestication in Nigeria of this imported American theology, eventually leading to the massive Americanization of both the Nigerian Charismatic movement and extending well into virtually every other sector of the Nigerian Church. One was the exodus of hundreds if not thousands of fledgling Nigerian pastors to Morris Cerullo's nine-month training sessions in America. While many such trainees settled permanently in America, a considerable number returned to Nigeria and planted hundreds of thriving churches, all of which boldly proclaimed Word of Faith theology. A second was the emergence of the Full Gospel Businessmen's Fellowship International in the late '70s, and a third was the annual visits and tours of Nigeria by young ministers from the Kenneth Hagin ministries in the early '80s.

All of this, we are suggesting, is behind a major theological transformation that has taken place in the Nigerian Church over the past generation. There was a massive importation of a seriously flawed theology that had been largely rejected by mainstream American Pentecostalism but that was eventually warmly embraced by ever-widening circles of not just neo-Pentecostal but eventually Pentecostal and even non-Pentecostal Nigerian churches.

Whether it was fully intended or not by men such as Kenyon and Hagin, what we are seeing here is the emergence of a singular quest for *material prosperity*, but within the framework of an unscriptural theology, as we will soon point out. Nigerians who had emerged from centuries of conditioning toward a holistic understanding of spiritual and material issues and who were deeply oppressed by the economic hell they were passing through in the '80s and '90s were drawn to this teaching like a magnet.

The sad result is that the Health and Wealth message has turned much of the Nigerian Church upside-down and has transformed God-centeredness into self-centeredness. It is not a minor development, but one with huge consequences. Our deep conviction is that the capturing of the lost revival vision of the '60s and '70s will not and cannot happen until we first experience a deep-down reformation that will sweep away the errors of the American Health and Wealth gospel. We must return to a sound foundation of prosperity teaching as found in the pages of the Holy Bible.

WHAT DOES THE BIBLE SAY ABOUT PROSPERITY?

Prosperity is an important Bible theme. However, a proper understanding of prosperity requires that we place it in the context of the overall message of God's revelation, both in the Old Testament and the New Testament. When we do that we discover that the imported American Health and Wealth or Word of Faith teaching substantially deviates from the Bible concept of prosperity and hence has become a major seducer of the Nigerian Church.[46]

The Bible teaching about prosperity can only be understood properly within the context of God's covenant with humankind. In the Old Testament the strongest underlying pillar of Hebrew thinking was the concept of the covenant struck between God and man. This covenant originated within the private councils of an eternal God who revealed it to mankind with His name *Yahweh*. The loving Yahweh's sovereign covenant with mankind is a pure product of His own unexplainable "loving kindness," or *hesed*. Therefore,

---

[46]Much of this section is dependent on a white paper produced by Dr. Vic Reasoner, an adjunct lecturer at West Africa Theological Seminary, Lagos, entitled *"Faith and Prosperity in Biblical Perspective."*

while God strongly desires prosperity for His people, he offers it to them strictly on His own terms..

This is why accepting the terms of God's covenant means unconditional surrender on our part. It is also why all of God's promises of prosperity are made to covenant keepers (e.g., Deuteronomy 28, Psalm 1:3; Proverbs 28:13). It is *if* we fully obey the Lord that we will become the head and not the tail (Deuteronomy 28:13). There is nothing in the Bible about *"naming it and claiming it,"* or about writing our own ticket with God.[47] Rather, as we follow a life of obedience to God's commandments we receive God-ordained blessings. To teach prosperity apart from covenant obedience is antinomian the belief that we can retain the favor and blessing of God no matter how we live. According to Malachi 3:10-12 God blesses those who tithe, but as a part of their covenant obedience to God. It is not the sowing of some kind of seed faith, but simple obedience to God, without which His blessings may not flow.

Jesus teaches that His followers are to totally depend on God for the provision of their material needs. He instructed them in Matthew 6:19-20 not to store treasures on earth but rather to store them in heaven. Part of His reason for this is that storing treasures on earth has a seductive tendency (verse 21). This is the fundamental flaw of focusing one's spirituality and religion on the material gain it will bring here and now. That focus inevitably corrupts as it galvanizes the individual to material needs and often to the detriment of spiritual needs.

---

[47]This is contrary to the teaching of Kenneth Hagin, who says we can literally *"write our own ticket"* with God. See Kenneth E. Hagin, *How to Write Your Own Ticket with God* (Tulsa, OK: Faith Library, 1979). Hagin says that in a personal encounter with Jesus he was told, *"If anybody, anywhere, will take these four steps* [say it, do it, receive it, and tell it] *or put these four principles into operation, he will always have whatever he wants from Me or God the Father"* (*Ibid*, p. 5).

It is in this context that Jesus enunciates the central issue regarding material prosperity. He makes it clear that material things are as important as the eye is to the body. However, we must ensure that the eye is good, correctly aligning the material in the overall scheme of things. If, on the other hand, our eye is bad, with material issues taking disproportionate space, we end up groping in spiritual darkness while all the time thinking we are in the light. This is a classical case of spiritual seduction. While agreeing that money and the materials it can buy are of considerable importance in life, we must be careful to get things in correct perspective.

Jesus teaches us not to worry, or to be unduly concerned about material things (Matthew 6:25-30). The reason is simple: God is our heavenly Father. Just as God provides for plants and birds, He will surely provide for us, His children. Therefore, worrying about material things demonstrates our lack of faith.

When we come to God *primarily* to meet our material needs we demonstrate how little we trust God (verse 30). Sadly, this is too often the case with the Nigerian Church. What we are taught by the Word of Faith teachers about the function of faith actually demonstrates our faithlessness. What Jesus is teaching us is that true faith is quiet acquiescence flowing from a confidence in the care of a loving Heavenly Father. But to the contrary, much of the prayers and rituals that Nigerian Christians engage in for material prosperity manifest how little they believe God deeply cares for them.

Jesus goes on to say that those who live and pray primarily in quest of material things are demonstrating that they are not Christians at all. For example, in Matthew 6:32 He notes that it is pagans who live that way not His true disciples. Surely that kind of teaching should cause us to carefully examine our own beliefs and practices. Bible Christianity demands that we have full confidence in a caring, loving Heavenly Father who knows our needs. This is what true matured faith means (Isaiah 30:15).

There are many reasons why this is extremely important. For one thing, it is only this type of mind-set that frees us to concentrate our energies on the kingdom of God. When our major attention is given to the pursuit of material things, even through bona fide spiritual means, we are seduced away from the focus on kingdom matters.

Getting in tune with God on these issues produces an amazing result. When we seek the kingdom of God and all its righteousness all our true needs will be met by our ever-caring Heavenly Father. This is the summation of Jesus' teaching on how we obtain our material needs. Our material needs are real and important, and God knows that and cares about that just as much as we do. However, rather than focus on them and how to meet them, we are instructed to focus on the spiritual matters that concern the kingdom of God and all its righteousness. When we use all our spiritual resources towards this end, God, in turn, as our Heavenly Father, will supply all our needs according to His riches in glory (Philippians 4:19).

EXPLOITING THE WEAK LINKS

We have seen the sharp contrast between the biblical teaching of covenant and prosperity and that of the American Health and Wealth or Word of Faith teaching.

But why, we must ask, has this false teaching had such a strong appeal for the Nigerian Church? Five basic reasons seem clear. And they expose to us the weak links that made it possible for such a massive seduction.

First, the strong emphasis of the message of the earlier revival period on the imminence of the Second Coming of Jesus and the fact that it did not materialize eventually shook the faith of many. A majority of those caught up in the revival were young and impressionable. Because of their urgent expectation of the return of Christ, many were willing to shelve material considerations for more eternal values. When it did not materialize as they had expected many of them began to question the validity of their focus. As they advanced in age many began to think more seriously about their temporal future. When this new Word of Faith message stressing the meeting of worldly needs began to come into clear focus many were ready to go along with it.

A second reason why the Word of Faith teaching proved so popular in Nigeria was a reaction to the Scripture Union as well as mainline Pentecostal leaders teaching, discouraging any focus on materialism, under the conviction that it undermined spiritual values. Instead, they had encouraged educational pursuits and white-collar jobs such as civil service, teaching and the professions. However, with few exceptions, business and politics were not encouraged as suitable for people interested in the welfare of their souls. This gradually made their teaching unpopular with the masses that were by the '70s and '80s beginning to see post-independence development as an opportunity for personal material gain.

A third factor is that as a result of this failure of many churches to understand the cry of the masses for material answers Christianity was relatively unpopular and not many were being attracted to the older churches. The emerging middle-class and the intelligentsia certainly had no interest in serious Christianity, which was seen as a promoter of poverty as well as consolation for social failure. As a result, some of the new teachers became persuaded that to attract significant numbers to Christianity it would be necessary to change the message. It would have to shift from one primarily focused on heaven to something catering to the aspirations and physical and material needs of the here and now.

Yet a fourth reason for the attraction of the Health and Wealth message, most especially in eastern Nigeria, is that the end of the Civil War brought with it a deep desire to make up for lost welfare and economic advancement. Those most negatively impacted by the war saw a primary need to focus on entrepreneurship. In order to attract this class of people to the church, there was a need to scratch them where they itched by presenting a message dealing with immediate material needs. Word of Faith teaching proved for many the right answer at the right time.

Finally, we must not ignore the fact that since time immemorial African culture, like most others, places a high value on material success. It is undeniable that in Africa a religion based on material success will always be likely to resonate with the masses. As revival fervor waned it became a progressively deeper conviction to many that the earlier revival emphasis majoring on the need to prepare for heaven was likely to keep Africa backwards and permanently underdeveloped.

Fatal Flaws and Disastrous Consequences

No matter how significant the factors may have been in the triumph of the Health and Wealth message in Nigeria it nonetheless falls short of biblical truth and balance. We believe there are four biblical or theological flaws that render Word of Faith teaching unworthy of perpetuation by the Nigerian Church. These fatal errors need to be acknowledged and corrected. We believe that once they are corrected the door will potentially swing open for a fresh spiritual revival in the country.

<u>Confusion about the nature of faith</u> lies at the heart of Word of Faith errors. In simple terms, Bible faith is *trust* in an omnipotent and sovereign God on the part of finite and dependent human beings. The faith of health and wealth teachers, by contrast, is a self-generated *force* through which people cause things to happen. The difference is enormous. One concept is theologically and scripturally sound, and the other is mistaken and biblically indefensible.

Charles Farah, who served many years as a Pentecostal professor at Oral Roberts University, spoke out against the errors of Word of Faith teaching forty years ago, stating that what was proclaimed as faith was in fact presumption. He noted, *"Failure to distinguish the difference between these two has caused untold anguish to thousands of sincere and dedicated Spirit-filled Christians for whom the ordinary formulas have not worked."* [48] The modern teaching of faith, he says, is based on presumption. It is essentially not faith in God but rather faith in our own self-generated faith. [49] Yet Jesus clearly taught that we were to have faith *in God* (Mark 11:22), not in our own faith. The object of our faith is extremely important, and the only worthy object is Almighty God!

Within the Word of Faith movement scriptures were often interpreted out of context and faulty exegesis was pawned off as sound scholarship. A glaring example was Kenneth Hagin's

[48] Charles Farah, *From the Pinnacle of the Temple: Faith vs. Presumption* (Plainfield, NJ: Logos, 1978), 205. Farah was Professor of Theology and Historical Studies at Oral Roberts University from 1967-1991 and from 1994-1995.

[49] For example, see Charles Capps, *How to Have Faith in Your Faith* (Tulsa: Harrison House, 1986).

often-repeated erroneous interpretation of Mark 11:22, which is properly translated *"Have faith in God."* Without any foundation in sound exegesis Hagin insisted that it should be translated, *"Have the faith of God."* The apparent reason was that Hagin's faulty theology called for a focus not on a faith dependent on and focused on God but a self-generated faith of similar character and power to God's own faith.

Shifting focus away from God to the act of faith itself is dangerous. We are told that since we share in the divine nature we, too, like God, can exercise self-generated and creative faith. Kenneth Copeland taught, for example, that *"God is a faith being"* and that man operates in the same way God operates. This is not scriptural. It robs genuine faith of its only proper object.[50]

Word of Faith teachers claim that through "creative words" we manufacture our own realities, using the power of positive confession. Yet what men like Copeland call "positive confession" is the same technique that the occult world calls "creative visualization." The key is that in both cases the focus is shifted away from God to man. It is not only based on a false understanding of the nature of biblical faith but it also veers dangerously into the realm of sorcery. It is teaching that is traceable to E. W. Kenyon and those who influenced him, and not to sound Bible interpretation.

As we have noted, Copeland describes faith as a *force* released by our words. Contrary to the scriptural focus on the omnipotence of Almighty God, Word of Faith teacher Charles Capps said, *"Words are the most powerful thing in the universe."* On the basis of this kind of false teaching we are told, for example,

---

[50]McConnell, *A Different Gospel* (Peabody, MA: Hendrickson, 1988), p. 141; see Kenneth Copeland, *The Force of Faith* (Fort Worth, TX: Kenneth Copeland Publications, 1983).

that we can by the force of our words create wealth. Sometimes Job 22:28 is cited as a biblical basis for decreeing wealth, where Eliphaz says, *"You will also declare a thing, and it will be established for you."* However, these are not only not the words of God Himself, but later on God declares that what Eliphaz had spoken was not right.

> **REALITY CHECK:** The Word of Faith movement undermines Bible teaching about faith. Bible faith is trust in an infinite and omnipotent God on the part of finite and dependent humans. Faith therefore never focuses on our own abilities or our own power but always on the ability and power of Almighty God.

The Bible contains over four hundred verses on the use and abuse of money. There are far more New Testament warnings about the dangers of wealth and its capacity to draw people away from God than there are positive commendations of wealth.[51] At any rate it is clear that wealth is to be gained by following biblical principles of stewardship - not through some kind of magic or power released by spoken words.

Yet Word of Faith teacher Charles Capps taught that we set in motion spiritual laws by what we say and that if applied correctly, everything we say will come to pass.[52] Thus, we are taught that we can command God and that he is obligated to provide wealth or to heal because of our confession of faith. A. A. Allen, another Word of Faith proclaimer, once boasted he could command God to turn dollar bills into twenty-dollar bills. However, renowned Assemblies of God scholar Gordon Fee saw the danger of such claims, and declared, "God *must* do *nothing!*" Rather, God is the one who gives commands and we

---

[51]McCain, *"Prosperity: A Biblical Perspective,"* p. 64.
[52]Capps, *The Tongue: A Spiritual Force* (Tulsa: Harrison House, 1976), 22; 131-132.

are the ones to obey *His* commands.

We believe that what we are dealing with here is the age-old distinction between magic and religion. Within religion and certainly within the Christian religion it is the responsibility of people to submit themselves to the will of God. By contrast, magic involves people commanding spiritual powers. Therefore, within the context of Bible Christianity we must always say, *"Thy will be done."* Magic, on the other hand, says, *"My will be done."* The focus of magic is on self, and it is easy in the contemporary Nigerian Church to cross the line from Bible Christianity to magic in a desire to achieve our own wishes. As Lois Fuller notes, *"In religion the spiritual powers are begged and they may not agree, but in magic, the powers are manipulated and it is always supposed to work. People often say that God created magic powers for them to use to solve their own problems."*[53]

Word of Faith teachers assert that God has set up universal laws regarding health and wealth, and that we activate these laws by speaking them out. For example, C. S. Lovett wrote that God's healing power is available *through our own mind* and we can trigger it by faith. As he says, *"If you had direct access to your unconscious mind, you could command any disease to be healed in a flash."*[54] This is a stark illustration of the difference between healing as taught by the Word of Faith movement and divine healing as revealed in the scriptures. The ultimate question is whether we heal ourselves by speaking healing into reality or

---

[53] Lois Fuller, *A Missionary Handbook on African Traditional Religion*, Nigeria Evangelical Missionary Institute, Africa Christian Textbooks, 1st edition, 1994; 2nd edition, 2001, pp. 82-83; on p. 105 Fuller notes further, *"Treating God as a source of power where the person says, "My will be done" rather than "Thy will be done," is wrong and can lead to demonic invasion of the person using it. The true power of God comes only through a personal friendship with God, which in turn comes only repentance, faith in Christ, surrender and holiness."* See also Richard Gehman, *African Traditional Religion in the Light of the Bible*, (Jos: Africa Christian Textbooks, First edition, 2001; 2013), pp. 53-54.

[54] C. S. Lovett, "The Medicine of Your Mind," *Personal Christianity Newsletter* (Aug 1979).

whether we are healed by a sovereign and God-initiatedtouch from Jehovah Rapha.

Closely related to this erroneous teaching about the nature of Bible faith is the concept of "seed faith" giving of money. The prosperity teaching on seed faith is that we can materialize our hopes of dreams of success, prosperity, and abundance by sowing our best financial seed. Passages such as 2 Corinthians 9:6-15 and Galatians 6:7-9 are often cited though seriously out of context. We are told that we have the potential within us and if we will release it, God will make it grow. Thus we are encouraged to put our faith to work, to take the leap of faith, and expect God to work. All too often we are told that giving beyond our means to a faith preacher, pastor or church leader activates such faith.

Yet if we understand the Bible we know giving should be motivated by thanksgiving for what God has given us, and never in anticipation of what God will give us. We do not give in order to receive. Matthew 6:38 does not imply "Give so that it will be given to you." Rather, it means that when we give to those persons or causes that are currently in need, others will give to us when our own time of need arises. We are not to turn giving into some sort of investment strategy as taught by Word of Faith teachers. In short, we can never force God to act in obligation to us. Giving is an act of obedience and an expression of worship, which should be the ultimate priority of the Church.

<u>Emphasis on continuing divine revelation</u> is a second major flaw in the Word of Faith movement. There is a thirst for "new" revelations and truths never before revealed. However, the final words of the Bible, in Revelation 22:18-19, tell us that God's revelation has closed. That God would wait hundreds of years and then start adding major postscripts is therefore not true. It is true that we all still need the Holy Spirit to illuminate God's Word, and to help us understand and apply it properly. And God can and does give personal guidance to His people. But the biblical and historic doctrine of sufficient revelation is that God has given to His Church all we need to know by way of revelation. The Bible is sufficient in and of itself as our deposit of divine truth. The Church needs no added revelation. Therefore, when we seek to know more than the Bible tells us, we only open ourselves up to potential deception.

Word of Faith teachers often raise confusion on this topic by over-stretching the distinction between *logos* and *rhema* in the scriptures. *Logos* is the recorded words of the Bible. *Rhema*, on the other hand, is said to be God's specific personal communication with His children here and now. We not only go by the Bible, but we also have fresh revelations from God that we can take *on a par* with scripture. Kenneth Hagin boldly talked about eight personal, literal, physical encounters with Jesus Christ, during some of which he says he was given specific and infallible revelations going beyond the teachings of scripture and which he regarded as sure and certain as the Bible itself.[55] This is highly questionable and dangerous teaching.

There is no doubt that one of the gifts of the Holy Spirit is that of prophecy. It is both the forth-telling and the fore-telling of the mind of God concerning an individual or a situation. Every mature Christian can and should be led by the Holy Spirit. This involves the capacity to receive guidance through the instruction of the Holy Spirit. An example of this is Paul's

---

[55]Kenneth E. Hagin, *I Believe in Visions* (Old Tappan, NJ: Fleming H. Revell, 1972).

experience in Acts 16:6-10. Not once or twice but three times, the Holy Spirit directly intervened in Paul's plans to guide him aright.

In some cases, God speaks through others who have the gift of prophecy. In Acts 21:10-11, Paul was warned by Agabus, a prophet from Judea, concerning the persecution that awaited him in Jerusalem.

Charismatic and Pentecostal believers generally hold that the gift of prophecy is valid in all ages, including our own. However the use of this gift has several scriptural restrictions. Some of them limit the number of people who can prophesy in a given meeting. Others insist that prophecies be judged and not necessarily taken at face value. The judgment of prophecy has to be based on correct scriptural interpretation.

Thankfully, we have a more sure word of prophecy. According to 2 Peter 1:20-21 the prophets of old were carried along by the Spirit of God as wind in the sails moves a boat along the water.

> *knowing this first, that no prophecy of Scripture is of any private interpretation, for prophecy never came by the will of man, but holy men of God spoke as they were moved by the Holy Spirit.*

Thomas C. Oden, who died in late 2016, told *Christianity Today* that he dreamed his epitaph would read: *He made no new contribution to theology.* This was expressive of a deep conviction with Oden. He noted that he had learned what the early Christian theologian Irenaeus meant

> *when he warned us not to invent new doctrine. This was a great discovery for me. All my education up to this point had taught me that I must be compulsively creative. If I was to be a good theologian I had to go out and do something nobody else ever had*

done. The dream somehow said to me that this is not my responsibility, that my calling as a theologian could be fulfilled through obedience to apostolic tradition.[56]

One of the great distractions used by Satan during the Civil War Revival was the extra-biblical revelation taught by Franklin Hall, Neil Frisby and William Branham. These men mesmerized their followers by claiming they had received new revelations directly from God that went beyond scripture urging their followers to stop bathing, to always pray with their eyes open, to run backwards, to expect to never die, to deny the trinity, etc. Frisby's insistence that God had revealed to him that Jesus Christ would return to earth soon in the vicinity of his Phoenix, Arizona church led to several gullible Nigerian university students dropping out of school and flying to Arizona to be on the front line of the rapture.[57]

> **REALITY CHECK:** The scriptures of the Old and New Testaments have always been regarded by Christian orthodoxy as sufficient and complete revelation for the Church. We are warned even within scripture to neither add nor subtract from God's written revelation. Religions or sects that allege new revelations from God that are necessary for full or better understanding of God's word to us are dangerous and should be avoided.

It is important for us to have a fresh understanding about this issue. When a leader or a church or a movement claim to be preaching things that have not been preached or understood or

---

[56] Kate Shellnutt, "Died: Thomas Oden, Methodist Theologian who Found Classical Christianity," *Christianity Today*, December 2016, http://www.christianitytoday.com/gleanings/2016/December. Accessed 15 December 2016.

[57] Matthews A. Ojo. *The End-time Army: Charismatic Movements in Modern Nigeria* (Trenton: NJ: Africa World Press, p. 2006), pp. 45-50; Gary S. Maxey, *Capturing a Lost Vision: Can Nigeria's Greatest Revival Live Again?* (Lagos, WATS Publications, 2016), pp. 129-130, 214-217.

revealed since the days of Bible we are on slippery ground. To imagine that everyone else has gotten it wrong but us over the centuries, including all of the great and anointed preachers of the past centuries, is the height of pride and a sure guarantee of error.

The idea of welcoming extra-biblical revelation was most strikingly introduced to Nigeria by the Latter Rain Movement, starting in the '50s. Among other teachings, they focused on the doctrine of "the manifest sons of God" that the Church would give rise to a special group of "overcomers" who will receive spiritual bodies and become immortal. For this and other reasons the Assemblies of God of the US deemed the Latter Rain Movement to contain heresy from the very beginning. On April 20, 1949, the Assemblies of God officially denounced Latter Rain teaching. Other established Pentecostal groups have passed similar resolutions.[58]

Many years after the rise and ebbing of the Latter Rain movement in Nigeria Sydney Elton said this:

> *In 1954, there was another attempt to establish through the Latter Rain [revival], the great kingdom teachings, and certain attempts were made particularly from America to go out to evangelise the Lord Jesus Christ and His gospel, but they also brought in the teaching of the kingdom as well. Then it became too commercialised, it became too much of a programme for various operators, not people who were dedicated to the glory of the Lord Jesus Christ but dedicated to the gathering in of dollars and the building up of individual churches and individual radio*

---

[58]Today the term "latter rain" is rarely used, yet influences from this movement are still present in the Nigerian Church. Modern movements such as the Brownsville/Pensacola Revival, the Toronto Blessing, and the "holy laughter" phenomenon are a direct result of Latter Rain theology. While many positive blessings have come from these movements it is nevertheless urgent that we distinguish what is wheat and what is chaff.

> *programmes. The motive was wrong and therefore the Holy Spirit was driven out of control of it.*[59]

The timely reminder here for all of us is that we must never become so caught up in attempts to discern the "new thing" that is happening or what we believe the "next move" of the Holy Spirit may be that we do not give adequate attention to biblical basics that may be eroding all around us. It was just too easy to forget that the Christian message must always be about the old, old story and not about some new revelation no one has ever heard before.

<u>The depreciation of Jesus Christ</u> is yet another dangerous flaw within the Word of Faith movement. Though it is surely not a directly intended consequence of their teaching, the net result is often that the work of Christ and the person of Christ is downplayed and diminished in the face of the anthropocentrism and material greed that are the natural outcomes of the Word of Faith teaching.

There are several leaders within the Word of Faith movement who teach that we are little gods and that like God we can create by speaking matter into existence. They talk as though man has merged with God. Kenneth Copeland says, *"You have the same creative faith and ability on the inside of you that God used when he created the heavens and the earth."* We can speak things into existence through our positive confession because we are in "God's class." He further says, *"You don't have a God living in you; you are one!"*[60] Such teaching has moved beyond scripture into serious error and confusion, and it also opens the door to a

---

[59]Sydney Elton sermon, "The Establishing of the Kingdom in Nigeria," Ayodeji Abodunde, *Messenger: Sydney Elton and the Making of Pentecostalism in Nigeria* (Lagos: Pierce Watershed, 2016) pp. 312-313.
[60]Kenneth Copeland, "The Force of Love," (Ft Worth: Kenneth Copeland Ministries, 1987), Tape #02-0028

serious depreciation or diminishing of the work and the person of Jesus Christ.

There has been a tendency to misunderstand the use of the Hebrew word *elohim* in the scriptures. For example, in John 10:34 Jesus quotes from Psalm 82:6 - *"Is it not written in your law, 'I said, "You are gods"'"?* The word *elohim* is the plural form of *el*, which means God. It occurs more than 2,200 times in the Old Testament, and almost always refers to God, the Supreme Creator. However, it is also used some 245 times to describe the gods of the heathen, or angels, or men of superior rank.[61]

For example, Psalm 82:1 says, *"God presides in the great assembly; he gives judgment among the gods."* Here "gods" refers clearly to magistrates, judges, and other people who hold positions of authority and rule. They are people who have authority over other human beings, whose authority is to be feared but who derive their power from God, who in verse 8 is seen as judging the entire earth.

When God told Moses he would make him like God to Pharaoh (Exodus 7:1) it meant that as God's messenger he would speak God's word to Pharaoh and be God's representative to him. It did not mean that Moses was in any sense God Himself or some kind of "little god." The lie of Satan in the Garden of Eden was that *"God knows that in the day you eat of it your eyes will be opened, and you will be like God, knowing good and evil"* (Genesis 3:5). But that was only a half-truth. Definitely their eyes were opened (v. 7), but they did not become like God. Satan deceived Eve about her ability to become like the one true God. Human beings are not "gods"

---

[61] W. T. Purkiser, Richard S. Taylor, Willard H. Taylor, *God, Man & Salvation: A Biblical Theology* (Kansas City: Beacon Hill Press of Kansas City, 1977), p. 53.

or even "little gods." We are not God. God alone is God, and those who are in Christ are God's children.

Speaking of the temptation to self-focus and the deification of man, Scot McKnight says that *"The story of sin in the Bible is the story of God's elect people wanting to be God-like instead of godly, of ruling instead of sub-ruling and being ruled."* McKnight further notes that in this light we can see that the essence of the fall of Adam and Eve is not only disobedience and original sin, but also the equally grievous sin - wanting to "be like God" [3:5].[62]

A sad corollary of this teaching is that many within the Word of Faith movement see God as our servant. In his excellent treatise on "The Need for Christian Theology and Sound Doctrine," Joseph Ali notes:

> *There are some wrong attitudes that have spread among full-gospel preachers today. They stem from the teaching that makes God our "servant-boy." Since God exists for man, (as some believe) and not man for God (as it should be), the true Christian value is down played in the drive to meet man's temporal needs.* [63]

According to Copeland, Christ performed miracles through the force of faith exercised by the authority of the words he used. His miracles were not necessarily because he was the Son of God but because he tapped into universal powers that exist independently from God. Therefore, Christ had no unique power that is not available to all Christian believers. This type of teaching quite clearly diminishes the person and power of Jesus Christ. He now becomes not the unique and

---

[62]Scot McKnight, *Kingdom Conspiracy: Returning to the Radical Mission of the Local Church* (Grand Rapids: Brazos Press, 2016), p. 28.
[63]Joseph Ali, *Earnestly Contending for the Faith: An Agenda for Responsible Christian Leadership, Second Edition* (Garki, Abuja: Concerned Ministers' Forum, 1999), p. 29.
Kevin Reeves, *The Other Side of the River* (Silverton, OR: Lighthouse Trails, 2007), 23, 27, 30, 121.

one-and-only Son of God but rather some kind "pattern Son" to be imitated by all the rest of us.

Copeland says Jesus walked on earth as an anointed man, empowered by the Holy Spirit, and that potentially all Christians now have this same anointing and can therefore do exactly what Jesus did. Benny Hinn joins in with his own teaching that we are little gods on the earth, and that all the fullness of God dwells in *us*, much as it did in Jesus(Col 2:9). These people, incidentally, are not talking about power or enablement from God to live a holy life, but rather power to, as they would say, "walk in the miraculous."[64] Frankly, this is destructive and seducing error even veering toward the blasphemous. At the least it is a serious affront to the person and the work of Jesus Christ, the one-and-only Son of God.

Kenneth Copeland goes on to say, *"You have the same creative faith and ability on the inside of you that God used when he created the heavens and the earth."*[65] If Jesus is born again as Copeland claims he is and is now exalted to the right hand of God, then we who are also born again are equal with Jesus Christ. We are incarnations of God through identification. We are so identified with Christ, we are so "in Christ," that we are equal with Christ. Thus, we are little gods and can create simply by speaking matter into existence.[66] But all of this is a million miles from Bible teaching about the uniqueness of the God-

---

[64]Kevin Reeves, *The Other Side of the River* (Silverton, OR: Lighthouse Trails, 2007), 23, 27, 30, 121.

[65] Kenneth Copeland, *Inner Image of the Covenant* (Fort Worth: Kenneth Copeland Ministries, 1985, audiotape #01-4406), side 2.

[66]Kenneth E. Hagin, *New Thresholds of Faith* (Tulsa, OK: Faith Library Publishers, 2ⁿᵈ ed., 1985 [1972], p. 56, E. W. Kenyon, *What Happened from the Cross to the Throne*, (Lynwood, WA: Kenyon's Gospel Publishing Society, 13ᵗʰ printing, 1969 [1945]), p. 62.; for a thorough analysis of the "born again Jesus" teaching see Judith A. Matta, *The Born Again Jesus of the Word-Faith Teaching*, (Fullerton, CA: Spirit of Truth Ministry, 1987).

man, Jesus Christ. We will never be equal with Him. He and He alone is the only begotten Son of God!

> **REALITY CHECK:** John the Baptist said, *"He must increase, but I must decrease"* (John 3:30). The diminishing of the person or ministry Jesus Christ has been one of the primary marks of false teachings down through the ages of Christian history. Word of Faith theology disqualifies itself as sound teaching when it seeks to increase finite humans and thereby decrease the Son of God.

We must never forget that when man is deified, Christ is diminished. Copeland taught that when Jesus went to the cross, he placed Himself in the hands of Satan and took on Himself Adam's sinful nature. According to Copeland and several others within the Word of Faith movement, Christ underwent a change of nature into a satanic being and completely lost His deity. Satan conquered Jesus on the cross and took His spirit to hell where He was tortured for three days. Jesus died spiritually, in the flaming fires of hell, and was thereafter born again, according to Copeland.[67] The born again Jesus then defeated Satan.

However, scripture does not affirm the teaching that Jesus Christ descended into hell to suffer nor has it ever been orthodox Christian teaching. His suffering was over and concluded when he declared, *"It is finished."* All of this teaching is far from the truth of the Bible. It is aberrant theology yet it is the kind of theology that even today continues to seduce the Nigerian Church.

---

[67]Kenneth Copeland, "The Price of It All," *Believer's Voice of Victory*, Sept, 1991, 3-6; E. W. Kenyon was the originator of the idea that Jesus died spiritually, as seen in his books, *What Happened From the Cross to the Throne* and *Identification: A Romance in Redemption* (as cited in D. R. McConnell, *A Different Gospel, Updated Edition* (Peabody, MA: Hendrickson Publishers, 1995 [1988], p. 117).

A fourth major area of error in the Word of Faith teaching is <u>the tendency to reduce prosperity to materialism</u>. Within this movement materialism is accumulating personal wealth and possessions as an end in itself. Therefore, it is inevitably married to the sin of greed. The Bible issues repeated warnings against the sin of greed and against the *"laying up of treasures on earth"*(Matthew 6:19-21). Paul tells us bluntly that greed is idolatry and that greedy people will not inherit the kingdom of Christ (Ephesians 5:5). Yet the seduction of the Nigerian Church has reached such a high level in our own day that material greed is frequently honored, cherished and shamelessly pursued, from the top of the Church all the way to the bottom. This sad syndrome is a direct result of the seduction of the American Health and Wealth teaching.

Nowhere is the devastation of the false doctrines of Word of Faith teaching more clear than in the loss of innocence, humility and integrity on the part of our leaders. Long gone is the humility and simple lifestyles we once knew in the persons of people such as Bishop Ajayi Crowther, Henry ("Holy") Johnson, and more recent exemplars during our Civil War period such as W. F. Kumuyi, Mike Oye, and even more mainstream leaders such as Francis Akanu Ibiam, along with many others. In their place these days are too many leaders marked more by pride, worldly sophistication and in several cases fabulous wealth.

Femi Aribisala decries the shamelessness of the private wealth and ostentation of many of Nigeria's health and wealth advocates, whom he labels "babalawo" pastors.[68] He cites Bishop David Oyedepo's claim that *"There's a proven covenant cure for poverty,"* despite Jesus' plain declaration that *"You will*

---

[68] Femi Aribisala, "Nigeria's 'Babalawo' Pastors," *Vanguard*, 28 April 2014.

always have the poor among you" (John 12:8), and the declaration of Deuteronomy 15:11 that *"The poor will never cease from the land."*

The fact that there are scores of pastors and church leaders within the Nigerian Church who measure personal wealth in millions of dollars, and not less than a half dozen who own private jets, is a staggering and embarrassing indictment against all of us. Virtually none of them have transparent financial accountability to their followers. Some who have ventured into extended ministries outside Nigeria where government surveillance over personal and church finances is more active have run afoul of authorities over accusations of financial exploitation and amassing illegal personal fortunes.[69] Let's face it: this is no longer the religion of the Bible or of Jesus of Nazareth.

Clearly, the Health and Wealth teaching usually works quite well for those who are able to position themselves at the top of the pyramid. But if the message of personal prosperity and freedom from debt and financial breakthrough were working as well as the prosperity preachers tell us, it would seem to us that by now the Nigerian economic realities would be different for those at the middle and lower levels as well. But poverty is still clearly the lot of not just a few Nigerians but of growing numbers, including indiscriminately among those who listen to and apparently accept the Health and Wealth message. In short, the message is being received but it is generally not working. Minds appear to be convinced, and hopes are again and again raised, but pocketbooks remain largely empty. The pressing question is, when are the masses

---

[69]Tim Cocks, "Nigeria's 'megachurches': a hidden pillar of Africa's top economy," Reuters, October 12, 2014, http://www.reuters.com/article/us-nigeria-megachurches-insight-idUSKCN0I104F20141012. Accessed 12 January 2017.

going to wake up and admit that this stuff is not working?

In 2006 *Christianity Today* published information questioning the foundational identity of global Pentecostalism. In an article entitled "What Really Unites Pentecostals?" Ted Olsen noted that it was no longer speaking in tongues that unites Pentecostals around the world, but rather the message of material prosperity. He noted that 95% of Nigerian Pentecostals agree that *"God will grant material prosperity to all believers who have enough faith."* And 97% agree that *"God will grant good health and relief from sickness to believers who have enough faith."*[70]

Yet we must be honest enough to admit that effective material prosperity still largely eludes the masses, including the vast majority flocking to hear the prosperity message. In the end all too often this false gospel is good only for an elite few, who seem to have opted out of the struggles of the masses around them while much too often contributing relatively little to the advancement of the heavenly kingdom.

One important question to ask here is that posed by Jesus Himself. In Mark 8:36-37 he asks what is worth exchanging for one's soul. Materialism presents itself as the route to true satisfaction. The more we have, the happier we are. That is common wisdom. However, in reality it is often not true. The quest for more possessions has the tendency to displace inner peace, and is a very poor substitute.

However, genuine prosperity results in inner peace and comes

---

[70] Ted Olsen, "What Really United Pentecostals?" *Christianity Today*, 50:12 (Dec 2006), p. 19. According to Isaac Phiri and Joe Maxwell, "Gospel Riches: Africa's rapid embrace of prosperity Pentecostalism provokes concern and hope," *Christianity Today*, July 2007, Vol. 57, No. 7, p. 26.

only in company with righteousness. It produces joy in the Holy Spirit (Romans 14:17). In other words, righteousness is the way to inner peace and joy. This deep inner contentment is what people most earnestly hope for in life.

Those who follow Christ as true disciples know that righteousness only comes when we are in a correct relationship with God. When we relate to God as our heavenly Father, we depend on Him to meet our needs. We accept what he chooses to provide with gratitude. This frees us to devote ourselves to the service of God's kingdom. The resulting feeling of peace and joy is priceless. It is this condition that truly constitutes prosperity. Unfortunately, however, multitudes of Nigerian Christians are today being fed with a false gospel that equates materialism with prosperity.

The sad truth is that it is easy for this kind of gospel to be preached at the expense of God's sovereignty and in ignorance of His desire to have a holy people (1 Peter 1:15-16). Even when other Bible themes are preached they tend to be drowned out in the ears of economically oppressed people by the promise of personal financial wealth here and now. The bottom line has all too often become a "seek-God-for-your-bread-and-butter" gospel."[71]

The contrast between this teaching and what obtained during the height of revival in the '60s and '70s could hardly be more dramatic. One could easily argue that in that earlier period there was an unbalanced and perhaps even unhealthy aversion to money and material goods, yet the pendulum has swung ridiculously far to an opposite and even greater error. We are now told that being poor is sinful, and that literally every Christian must be rich. We are told that *"Whatever is not of faith is*

---

[71]Ali, *Op cit*, pp. 30-31.

sin" (Romans 14:23), and that therefore since faith is the assurance of things hoped for and the realization of things not seen, (Heb. 11:1) to be poor is to not exercise faith, and therefore it is sinful and advertising God in a bad light.[72]

It is to be feared that in the modern Nigerian Church much of the membership have come to the conclusion that Christianity is basically all about material prosperity. Wealth is in many sectors projected as a sign of spirituality. Faith in Christ is quantified most readily in material terms. On the other hand, poverty is a curse. Churches with those messages are attracting ever-larger audiences as they focus their message on how to "prosper" and to get their next "breakthrough." Scriptures that focus on self-sacrifice, self-denial, the cross, sin and holiness are seldom used. When members of such churches "prosper," almost never does anyone ask after the genuineness of their sources of wealth. [73] Onofurho notes,

> *Let us observe some common traits of such preachers: their churches are more of a family enterprise. Every worker is actually working for their family. They are proud and flamboyant in their lifestyle. They are hardly approachable. They can hire and fire staff at will. They own a number of cars when their immediate assistants have none. Their preaching is more emotional than spiritual. When one is asked to sow a seed of faith, he ends up sowing into the preacher's pocket.* [74]

Consonant with this unbalanced perspective is the further idea that Christians must never suffer. As the popular chorus says, *"Me I no go suffer, I no go beg for bread."* Because God is our Father

---

[72] Victor Ogunkanmi, Contending, *Earnestly Contending for the Faith: An Agenda for Responsible Christian Leadership, Second Edition* (Garki, Abuja: Concerned Ministers' Forum, 1999), p. 81.

[73] Onofurho, *Contending*, p. 55.

[74] Onofurho, *Challenges of the End-Time Church*, pp. 55-56.

and owns the entire universe and loves us dearly, and because suffering comes from lacking things, and because God will always provide for us, therefore we must never suffer. Yet suffering is an unavoidable part of Christian life. God at times allows His beloved children to suffer. James in fact tells us that we should count it all joy when we fall into suffering and troubles because of the testing of God and God's design to bring us out to a better end. Suffering for God is a central part of Christian experience. [75]

Part of the fallout from false theologies regarding suffering is that in general the southern Church in Nigeria is ignoring the calamitous decimation of their Christian brothers and sisters in Northern Nigeria. Rather than embracing the stark truth that unbelievable suffering and record-breaking Christian martyrdom is faced every day just a few hundred miles north of them, it is drowned out by an ignorant quest for comfort and prosperity. Or, worse yet, there is nurturing of hatred and vengeance toward Muslims.

There is also a marked failure of theological schools to adequately address the issues at a biblical and theological level and to provide the leadership that is so desperately lacking within the Church. Jan Boer has written extensively on this topic, in an attempt to enlighten a Nigerian public that is usually shielded from the facts. Yet a southern Church filled with its incessant quest for prosperity responds with deafening silence. [76]

Health and Wealth teaching in Nigeria has gradually destroyed

---

[75] Ogunkanmi, *Contending*, p. 84.

[76] Jan H. Boer, *Nigeria's Decades of Blood 1980 2002* (Belleville, Ont: Essence Publishing, 2004), volume 2 of 8 in the "Studies in Christian - Muslim Relations" series, available free of charge www.SocialTheology.com.

biblical concepts of stewardship. A whole generation of Nigerian church goers have become convinced that the primary purpose of giving is to receive. They believe that *"the anointing paves the way to wealth."* [77] Luke 6:38 is wrenched out of context. Jesus noted, *"Give, and it will be given to you: good measure, pressed down, shaken together, and running over will be put into your bosom. For with the same measure that you use, it will be measured back to you."* However, Jesus is saying nothing about the God-ordained *motive* for giving, but rather that personal generosity has a way of generating reciprocal response. Our modern prosperity advocates, however, jump on this concept with passion and tout it as a primary motive for giving.

We have earlier pointed out the fact that Sydney Elton in his later years regretted and repudiated the excesses of persons and movements that he had earlier endorsed and encouraged. The same thing can be said of Archbishop Benson Idahosa, who in the final years of his life could be heard on numerous occasions discouraging the legions of imitators around him from putting too much focus on material gain. In both cases the concerns of these men fell largely on deaf ears.

According to Abodunde,

> *Elton was convinced that Idahosa had become negatively influenced by a stream of the Pentecostalism movement in America that was unduly emphasizing materialism and fame. Elton believed that certain wrong influences were beginning to*

---

[77] David Oyedepo, *Anointing for Breakthrough*, 1992, 2014 reprint, Dominion Publishing House, p 150; Oyedepo notes that *"on the 26th August 1987 while away on a mission trip to the United States the Holy Ghost delivered yet another task to me saying 'Get back home and make my people rich.' This command was so strong and compelling that I had to abandon all my scheduled meetings and rushed back to Africa."* David Oyedepo, *The Mandate Operational Manual, Living Faith Church Worldwide a.k.a. Winners Chapel International*, Foreword by David O. Oyedepo, 2012, Dominion publishing House, p. 97.

> *shape Idahosa's spiritual outlook   influences that would bring about a conversion to the American brand of Pentecostalism which Elton was wary of and had continually warned against.* [78]

In fairness to Kenneth Hagin, the father of the Word of Faith movement, we likewise note that before his death in 2003 he rebuked some of his own successors. He not only called several of them together to issue his rebukes but later wrote a book about it, entitled *The Midas Touch* in which he wrote that financial prosperity is not a sign of God's blessing, that we should never give in order to get, and that it is not biblical to "name your seed" in an offering. He specifically denounced the misuse of the "hundredfold return" concept that one could expect to receive one hundred dollars in return for every one dollar of offering. He warned that those claiming to have a "debt-breaking" anointing had no scriptural authority behind it and should not be trusted. Hagin was unhappy that his followers had manipulated the Bible to support what he saw as greed and selfish indulgence.

Yet Hagin could not deny the fact that his unbalanced and unscriptural teachings about faith had laid a foundation for the very things that his successors were teaching. It only served to illustrate the fact that when we deviate from the clear teaching of the Bible the departure from truth will inevitably lead to an ever-growing distance between error and truth. The only proper answer is to go back and correct the original misinterpretation of scripture and resulting false teaching.

---

[78] Ayodeji Abodunde, *Messenger: Sydney Elton and the Making of Pentecostalism in Nigeria,* (Lagos: PierceWatershed, 2016), p. 311.

> **REALITY CHECK:** The conviction of the Christian Church throughout the centuries is that God desires and promises to prosper His people by endowing them with Christlike character and pouring out blessings on them in response to their acceptance of His covenant. The scriptures affirm that God's covenant blessings are adequate to preserve His people through the toughest of circumstances. But the Word of Faith attempt to define God's prosperity as primarily material has pushed the Nigerian Church back toward an earlier ATR over-focus on this world.

Our earnest prayer is that God will deliver the Nigerian Church from the unbridled greed that has consumed us, from stem to stern. Peter Ozodo notes,

> *Some people claim that focusing the Church's message totally on the things of this world is the way to be relevant to the listener's needs. They claim that this is what will bring about Church growth. As a result, many have modified the gospel to fit the world. There is no more emphasis on the need for thorough repentance. Rather than teach holiness, many harp endlessly on materials gains. Some have gone to the extent of being carried away into seeking powers from forces other than God to enable them satisfy and influence their audiences. All that seem to count are methods that produce results. No one cares to know whether or not such methods square up with the Scriptures. The important thing seems to be that once the methods work, the people will keep coming. That guarantees for them positions and influence that will satisfy their ego. Our position is that, focusing on materialism causes Christian leaders to become worldly. . . . By listening to it, many have become pseudo-Christians, clinging to worldly materialism and remaining totally untransformed.*[79]

---

[79]Ozodo, *Op cit*, pp. 10-11.

The Nigerian Church stands in need of revival. We need to earnestly capture the lost vision of national spiritual awakening. The Holy Spirit yearns over this nation to see that very thing happen. But until we find a way of repentance over the pursuit of the golden calf of unbalanced prosperity that revival will continue to elude us. There is surely a way through to God's victory, and we thank God for those who are prepared to pay the price to see it happen!

The Fatal Attraction of African Traditional Religion

A second major factor in the seduction of the Nigerian Church is the reviving of African Traditional Religion, or ATR. Despite earlier predictions and expectations to the contrary, ATR is alive and growing within Nigeria. At the time of Nigeria's independence from colonial rule, in 1960, there was speculation in some circles that ATR was on its way toward extinction as a factor in the religious landscape of Nigeria and the rest of modern Africa. It appeared to some that Islam and especially Christianity were destined to triumph to the point of pushing ATR out of the arena. Yet African Traditional Religion is stronger today than it was a few decades ago and especially when taking into consideration its revival within the Nigerian Church.

One of the theses of this book is that the Nigerian Church as a whole has yet to overcome or successfully replace the African Traditional Religion mindset. We must tread carefully here, of course, because human culture is morally neither inherently good nor inherently bad. Christianity is transcultural in the sense that it affirms and adapts to any aspects of human culture that are not contrary to its moral and spiritual principles, while at the same time displacing aspects of culture with which it is not in agreement. Therefore, the African mindset in and of itself is morally neither good not bad.

However, there are certain aspects of the African mindset that are incompatible with the biblical worldview. As a result, Christianity as practiced by a large percentage of Nigerian church-goers is heavily influenced by thinking that in important aspects remains contrary to the Christian scriptures and is carried over from long centuries of ATR thinking and practice.

What we are discussing here is not peculiar to Africa alone, of course. It is also true of many other cultures around the world as Christians within those cultures seek to evangelize and disciple their own people. There is always a tendency for unscriptural cultural traditions and practices to be carried over into national churches whether in Africa, Asia, Europe or the Americas.

These are heavy charges, but we believe they are true. And there is a direct link here with the subject of our last chapter. As we briefly noted in that chapter, one of the primary reasons Word of Faith teaching has gained such remarkable currency on the African continent is that it has exploited and adapted to the age-old worldview of African Traditional Religion. Both ATR and the Word of Faith movement are heavily self-focused man-centered thinking that clearly contrasts with the ethos of the Bible.[80]

---

[80]Richard Gehman expands on John Mbiti's affirmation that ATR is anthropocentric rather than theocentric, noting, *"African Traditional Religion centres on man. The whole emphasis is upon man gaining power needed to live a good life. Life centres on man and his interests and needs. . . . it is as if God exists for the sake of man,"* Richard Gehman, *African Traditional Religion in the Light of the Bible*, Africa Christian Textbooks, First edition, 2001; 2013, pp. 35, 234, 246.

THE ATR WORLDVIEW

There are important similarities between the worldview of African Traditional Religion and the worldview of the Bible. In fact, it is arguable that the traditional African worldview is closer to the worldview of the Bible than is the western, secular worldview. This is why the worldview of western societies, deeply affected by 18th-century Enlightenment reason and secularism, in many cases proved a hindrance rather than a help to the missionary forces bringing the Gospel in the nineteenth century to Nigeria. The typical failure within the western worldview to appreciate the practical reality and importance of the invisible spirit world was often like a dragging weight slowing down missionary progress.[81]

For Western missionaries, relationship with God was mostly in the realm of ideas, while for the African, it was in the domain of the pragmatic. It had to do with solving practical day-to-day existential problems. The tendency of many missionaries to either ignore or in some cases directly oppose the preoccupation of Africans with the spirit world left many new African believers in confusion and in most cases with deeply embedded syncretism.

It is important that we have a thorough understanding of the worldview imbibed by Africans over the past centuries. Unlike the two-tiered universe understood by most westerners, the typical worldview of African Traditional Religion conceives of

---

[81]In our generation this fact has been made widely known through the scholarship of missiologists/anthropologist Paul G. Hiebert, whose landmark article "The Flaw of the Excluded Middle" was first published in *Missiology: An International Review 10*, (January 1982): 35-47 and reprinted in *Anthropological Reflections on Missiological Issues* (Baker Books, 1994), 189-201.

the universe in three or four tiers.[82] At the top is the creator God, who is assumed to be benevolent but who is remote and largely inaccessible. Below that is the realm of angels and demons and the realm of ancestral spirits, which are conceived as dwelling in either one tier or two. At the bottom is the visible created world inhabited by human beings. All variations within African Traditional Religions fit within this pattern, though we are talking about literally thousands of distinct belief systems around sub-Sahara Africa, each with its minor variations.

The ATR worldview has no place for atheism. Unlike in the West, Africans almost never question the existence of God. Moreover, virtually all manifestations of ATR are monotheistic, in the sense that there is only one creator God at the apex. Africans do not traditionally communicate with the Creator God, because he is understood to be too far away. He is separated from them by the invisible spirit world the more remote realm of angels and demons and the closer realm ancestral spirits.

The challenge within this African worldview is therefore how to manipulate or handle or appease the unpredictable realms of ancestral spirits and angelic and demonic spirits to enable one to experience the care and benevolence of the creator God. The appeasing of ancestral spirits and defeating of evil or demonic spirits hence becomes a primary motivation within religion. That appeasement can involve sacrifices, pouring of libations, and employment of shamans (priests) or witch

---

[82] It is not necessary to think of these tiers in spatial terms. Referring to terms like "top," "middle" or "bottom" is not to be taken literally. Philippians 2:10 says, *"that at the name of Jesus every knee should bow, in heaven and on earth and under the earth"* belying the basic biblical worldview as comprised of three parts, but in this case with the "middle" tier described as "under the earth."

doctors with special power to counteract or appease evil spirits or forces and to attract benevolent spirits. A powerful shaman can tell one how to appease the angry spirits of the ancestors and what rituals need to be performed to counteract the demonic or human powers that are bent on harm or destruction.

Within this worldview any kind of human calamity is normally responded to not with *what* questions but with *who* questions. *Who* caused my illness? Was it an angry and neglected ancestor? Was it a demon? Or perhaps was it another living person who tapped into those powers and used them against me? Likewise, who is preventing me from getting married, or who is preventing me from getting pregnant? Who is preventing my promotion at work, or perhaps even from getting a job in the first place? Who is preventing the failure of my business? Traditionally those questions are asked of a shaman, who can then peer into the invisible spirit world and determine the source of the problem and lay out an effective response to ward off evil and attract a positive response.

Whichever way, the power of the shaman is usually not in explaining truth but in creating a fog of frenzy and fear. He is surrounded by mystery and holds power over people through his ability to make contact with the demonic world and to make his demands until finally deliverance is proclaimed, though it always comes at a price which is both monetary or material and also spiritual.

Why Has Pentecostalism Succeeded in Nigeria?

If we understand the traditional African mindset we can also understand why Pentecostalism has been so highly successful in places such as Africa. We have already pointed to the remarkable success of the Pentecostal movement in Nigeria. It is a success mirrored as well in the rest of Africa and several other areas of the globe outside the West. Much of the reason for this phenomenal success is that Pentecostalism takes quite seriously the reality of the invisible spirit world. Not only so, but Pentecostalism also takes seriously the active power of God in response to human physical and material needs. To a large degree Pentecostalism provides the missing link that was not there with many of the early missionaries.

Historic Pentecostalism has gained global attraction for the past 100 years by delivering a simple but profoundly relevant message that the power of God is available here and now in real and palpable ways. Miracles are therefore not merely to be read about in the Bible but to be experienced today. Physical healing is available on a daily basis not merely through medical science but even more importantly through the power of the Holy Spirit. Such a message, accompanied in many instances by the mysterious reality of speaking in tongues, has had a broad appeal in Nigeria and elsewhere especially to the needy keenly aware of their need for help from above.

Pentecostalism successfully stepped into the yawning gap left by the disconnect between the worldview of the first expatriate Christian missionaries of the nineteenth century and the worldview of Nigerians. The focus of Pentecostalism on the power of God and their affirmation of the reality of the spirit world was a formula for acceptance and success. I (Gary) have told elsewhere of the perceptive words of my first African mentor, within days of my arrival in Nigeria in 1982: *"The early missionaries gave us the Bible, but they did not teach us about the power in the blood of Jesus.* "[83] He greatly appreciated the fact that the Bible was the primary transforming agent in the establishment of the gospel in Africa. But he also knew that the failure of a majority of the earliest missionaries to teach Bible truths about the spirit world and the power of Jesus Christ over that world had created a major problem. He was aware that the majority of discipleship programs did not deal effectively with the converts' fear of and bondage to demonic powers. [84]

Though it was a gradual process, the introduction of Pentecostal theology into Nigeria to a large degree lessened the long-standing tendency toward Nigeria's awkward syncretism. For well over 100 years that syncretism has left many Nigerian Christians caught in the middle between their Bible-focused Christian faith and their desire to find satisfying answers to their power struggles with the invisible spirit world. Jesus truly has all power or authority in heaven and on earth (Matthew 28:18), and that includes *"authority to trample on serpents and scorpions, and over all the power of the enemy"* (Luke 10:18). In short, we do not hesitate to say that Pentecostalism has boldly addressed some of the greatest felt needs of the African heart and mind.

---

[83] Gary S. Maxey, *The WATS Journey: A Personal Narrative* (Lagos: WATS Publications, 2014), p. 43. Lois Fuller further notes that any religion that focuses primarily on heaven and the rewards of the after-life may not have enough attraction to supplant African Traditional Religion. *"Because ATR tends to be 'people-centered' and 'this world centered,' a religion whose main benefits are in the next life will not replace ATR. It might only be added to ATR. ATR will still be used for help in this life while Christianity might be seen as mainly for help in the next life. The power of Jesus over the powers of evil right now, means much more to people in an ATR background."* Lois Fuller, *A Missionary Handbook on African Traditional Religion*, Nigeria Evangelical Missionary Institute, Africa Christian Textbooks, 1st edition, 1994; 2nd edition, 2001, p. 122.

[84] Lois Fuller, *Op cit.*, p. 6.

THE BRIDGE TO THE CHURCH

It is quite to be expected that African culture should influence the practice of Christianity in Africa. As we have already explained, Christianity permits such influences to the extent that they do not contradict biblical teaching. It however becomes a problem when aspects of culture that are decidedly anti-scriptural influence the practice of Christianity.

An example of this in Europe, America and other Western countries is the widespread acceptance of such practices as divorce outside biblically approved limitations, and the accommodation of homosexuality not only among ordinary Christians but also among the clergy. These are clearly practices that do not conform to scriptural teachings yet are nowadays permitted by many Western churches. It is an example of the seduction of Christianity in those countries.

In Nigeria, the crossover into the Church of elements of cultural belief and behavior that are biblically offensive did not take place rapidly. We have already noted that Western missionaries who brought Christianity to West Africa sought to prevent such influences but carried their protections too far. They gave the impression that to become authentically Christian it was necessary to drop African culture as much as possible and totally embrace Western ways. To a large extent this slowed down the effective spread of their message. It also eventually led to what amounted to a rebellion by some of their followers who set up first Ethiopian churches and later Aladura churches.

These African "rebels" were only reacting to the extremes of the protectionist tendencies of the missionaries over Christian practice. Once they had set up their own churches, these new African church leaders were freed to express Christianity in a more authentically African manner. It is unfortunate but not surprising that in that process there were occasional serious errors in some of the beliefs and practices that they tolerated. They had not as adequately sifted the African mindset, beliefs and practices with the scriptures, as they should have. The result was that in setting up what they considered to be authentic African expressions of Christianity they in certain vital areas permitted it to be more African than Christian.

These sincere religious innovators adopted African musical motifs complete with drumming and hand clapping, which had been largely outlawed by early Western missionaries. They practiced a form of Christianity that sought to deal with existentialist problems with which Africans grappled but which had been ignored by the early missionaries. These included dealing with spiritually induced problems, confronting witchcraft, and healing the sick through prayers. None of these practices was out of tune with the scriptures.

However, there were other areas where they clearly went beyond scriptural limits. In some cases leadership patterns drew more from African Traditional Religion than from the scriptures. Leaders often became more like traditional priests who were go-betweens to the spirit world. People came to them for spiritual intervention. As a result, the concept of the universal priesthood of all believers and the scriptural ability of ordinary Christians to take problems directly to God was discouraged and suppressed. Therefore, the greater the problem, the more the need was felt to seek out these spiritual specialists for consultation and intervention.

The worst outcome of this situation is that the ordinary Christian was not discipled to grow in faith. As long as there was a strong man of God to mediate between him and God, all was well. Indeed, many went so far as to feel that there was no need for personal holiness. To obtain relief from their existential problems, all they needed was to go to the spiritual leader, offer whatever was prescribed for the sacrifices and perform whatever rituals were decreed.

Other carry-over beliefs include the fact that these problems were often understood to be brought about by evil spirits or evil people. Virtually no problem was seen as emanating by any source other than from malevolent persons or spirits. Most important of all, relationship with God was seen as merely transactional rather than transformational. One went to God to get problems solved rather than to be changed by God and brought into a living fellowship with Him, on the foundation of shared character.

The crossover of these and other Aladura practices into mainline Christian denominations has been a major contributory factor to the seduction of the Nigerian Church. It has been a slow but steady process. It began harmlessly enough through the gradual acceptance of aspects of Aladura practices in the mainline churches. These included the singing of songs more reflective of African music, complete with drumming and hand clapping. They became easily accepted first in some of the Western planted Pentecostal churches. Then by the late '70s such practices had become acceptable in Anglican and other Protestant churches. The Catholics were not far behind.

It was however the gradual sipping of the more unscriptural beliefs and practices that was to especially mark the seduction of the Nigerian church. During the Civil War revival, there was a strong emphasis on Bible study. Prayers were mainly focused on the quest for personal transformation. The spiritual development of those who had experienced the new birth was the hallmark of the growing revival. The focus of the expectation of most people was on the soon return of the Lord Jesus Christ. Material prosperity and the belief that human enemies and evil spirits were mostly responsible for the existential problems facing people were almost nonexistent.

However, when the Lord did not return as soon as many young Christians were expecting, other beliefs and practices gradually began to creep into the revival movement. They came mainly through those of the leaders who had been influenced by African culture but had not had the training or experience to sift these cultures adequately with the scriptures. For them, pragmatism was what mattered. If it worked, then it was acceptable. Conformity to scriptural guidelines was not given priority in the formulation of practices. One of the most important tests of whether a particular practice worked well was the extent to which it drew in more followers.

To be sure, some of these excesses were resisted by a good number of the revival leaders. For example, in the early '70s, the Scripture Union headquarters barred all those who promoted Pentecostal practices from leading Scripture Union meetings. Unfortunately, though, the effect of their regulation was that the baby was thrown out with the bath water. The practices that they prohibited did not sufficiently discriminate between what was biblical from what was not. It appeared to most observers to be primarily an effort at limiting Pentecostal influence.

It is regrettable that those who left the Scripture Union because of these restrictions included some who did not have the training or experience to ensure that the practices permitted under their leadership were completely scriptural.

Indeed, some of the new leaders had come into the revival movement directly out of Aladura churches. The result was that some practices that were more influenced by aspects of African culture that retained traditional religious traits crept in. It is regrettable that in these groups, relationship with God was mostly based on what people could get from Him rather than on the change He could bring about in them.

Since these tendencies were authentically African, they appealed to many and resulted in the rapid growth of these churches. The major draw factor was that these churches produced manifest results. Whether it was healing, deliverance, obtaining of jobs, promotions, securing of contracts, marriages or the birth of babies to previously barren parents, prayers were being visibly answered in these groups. Therefore, whatever beliefs or practices they promoted were seen as acceptable. The lack of accountability of some of these new leaders also meant that they were free to do whatever they thought was best. As long as it drew more members, anything would seem acceptable.

TIPPING THE SCALES IN THE WRONG DIRECTION

All of this notwithstanding, however, we would not be telling the whole story if we failed to note the negative contributions made by the importation of American fringe Pentecostalism represented by the Word of Faith movement. It should not surprise is that this importation tipped the scales in the wrong direction even with respect to this matter of careless acceptance of unscriptural practices from African culture.

The contemporary Pentecostal/Charismatic movement in Africa has at times taken negative elements of the African religious worldview and has baptized them with wrongly applied Bible verses and Christian language. There is resultant confusion as we try to understand and explain what is going on in the realm of the living dead (ancestral spirits) and demonic spirits. Contrary to scriptural teaching, for example, there is talk of demons becoming spirit husbands and wives. On the other hand, generational curses are spoken about with authority that is not clearly backed by sound scripture.

It is to be feared that in some instances the Christian "man of God" has replaced the age-old shaman or witch-doctor. African respect for their leaders is important and is to be accepted and encouraged. Yet it is easy for the pendulum to swing too far. Too often it is assumed that the man of God has peculiar powers given to him that he alone possesses. These powers presumably enable him to break through the second and third tiers of ancestral and demonic powers in a way that is not possible for others. This explains why in many instances followers flock by hundreds and even thousands and tens of thousands to some of Nigeria's top church leaders. It explains why people in the audience sometimes struggle to either touch them, sit where they have sat, or grab onto anything they have physically handled. At the very least this calls for a more thorough discussion about the boundaries between what is scriptural, what is cultural, and what may be leaning too far toward ATR.

We also need to consider seriously the primary goal we, as a Church, are trying to achieve and how the New Testament Church achieved it. As we have earlier pointed out, the fundamental objective of the Church is to take the message of the gospel to the whole world. It does not seem that the achievement of this goal is advanced by practices that almost deify some men of God to the detriment of enhancing the priesthood of the ordinary believer.

It is true that we do find New Testament instances where people sought to touch the apostles and objects that they might have touched, yet never in such a way that the apostles deflected glory from God Himself. The question we need to ask for then and for now is to what extent did these practices promote the spiritual transformation of the beneficiaries of such events? Was it and is it possible, indeed likely that such people could experience such miracles and still remain in their sins? On the other hand, if we emphasize principles and practices that enhance the ability of the ordinary Christian to impact his community through their changed lives, it is more likely that the impact would be more eternally enduring.

Specifically, how do we understand in the light of our own situation passages such as Acts 5:15-16 and Acts 19:11-12? In the Acts 5 passage, during the earliest days of the Jerusalem Church, sick people were brought out into the streets and laid on pallets so that the passing shadow of Peter would fall on them. As a result they were *"all healed."* In Acts 19, during Paul's ministry in Ephesus, God worked *"unusual miracles"* by Paul so that even handkerchiefs or aprons that he had touched were given to the sick and *"the diseases left them and the evil spirits went out of them."*

We must not overlook the fact that Luke repeatedly makes it clear that the healing power present both with Peter and Paul was from God and not from themselves or from any material objects. He does this in part by contrasting these reports with the false healing going on by pagans around them, as we see in Acts 8:9-11 and 19:13ff. Also, there is absolutely no indication that either Peter or Paul was initiating practices that were intended to become a norm for the Church, and indeed these are both very one-off incidents that Luke describes as "unusual."

The challenge here is for us to maintain a clear focus on what is distinct about Christianity and about the scriptures. There are many religions that address the need for physical healing and for power to overcome evil forces, but unlike other religions Christianity also offers heaven's solution to the problem of sin and separation from God. That is the primary distinctive of the Christian gospel.

Yet it has become easy for some within the contemporary Nigerian Church to overlook the issue of the salvation of the soul, and to play down seeking for peace or pardon from God. Preparation for a holy heaven and instruction on how to live a holy life and to then move out in service in the power of the Holy Spirit is too often relegated to secondary status or even altogether ignored. Rather, the issue is simply to get the all-powerful "man of God" to release his power to provide primarily solutions for physical and materials needs, by praying for them, anointing them, or simply touching them.

We must acknowledge that this represents a subtle but significant shift within Christianity. Great men of God of previous generations persuasively and with Holy Spirit anointing proclaimed the word of God. They were powerful men in the pulpit, or in speaking to the masses in the open fields. They were purveyors of God's truth. They sought for their audience to be changed into godly people much more than they sought for their material wellbeing, even when ministering among people of extreme poverty. Very importantly, they were also exemplars of Christian holiness who spent years digging into the scriptures but who also lived transparently godly lives.

Within the Nigerian Church much of that has changed. In many circles the focus is now primarily on the man of God not so much as a purveyor of truth over which he has labored for long hours but as priests who convey the physical and material blessings of God upon the people. Nowadays in Nigeria those who come to the man of God are not so much looking for truth or for understanding or to see models of righteous living as they are for "deliverance" or "breakthrough." They are not seeking for a better relationship with God but rather for the betterment of their personal lives.

If we understand the teaching of passages such as Ephesians 1:18-2:6 and if we appreciate the Protestant principle of the priesthood of all believers, we will teach our people that even the weakest child of God among us has access to the power of God over Satan and demons, and can be taught to wield those powers effectively. It is because as believers we are all seated at the right hand of Jesus, *far above all principality and power and might and dominion, and every name that is named, not only in this age but also in that which is to come*" (Ephesians 1:21). This is also why Jesus sent out the seventy in Luke 10 (not just His close disciples but a broad range of those following Him) and assured them that they all had *"authority to trample on serpents and scorpions, and over all the power of the enemy"* (Luke 10:17-20).

However, too often in the contemporary Nigerian Church the picture we are asked to see is that God desires to bless His people but that there is need for someone with special powers to help them break through the layers of opposition interposing between man and God. "Breakthrough" and "deliverance" are now the key words. They have gradually come to be seen more and more in simple economic or physical rather than essentially spiritual terms. And they have replaced "preaching" or "proclamation" and "revival" or "holiness" as our most important themes.

This also helps us understand that prayer in the Nigerian Church has progressively become less of communion, confession and humble supplication before a benevolent God and more of literally battling with demons. All too often our prayers begin with addressing God but soon shift to addressing not God but evil spirits both real and imagined. Much time is spent binding spirits, casting out spirits, burning spirits with fire, and opposing and commanding spirits in every conceivable way. In turn, we loose the Holy Spirit and we decree this and that blessing on friends and curses on foes. There is no scriptural basis for such practices. Indeed, there is no scriptural basis for such often-popular mantras as *Holy Ghost fire* with which people often attempt to ward off evil forces.

Reference is often made to Daniel's experience in Daniel 12 where the angel told him that the Prince of Persia had intercepted the answer to his prayer. However, Daniel's involvement in bringing change to the situation was more passive than active. He continued in his fasting and prayers because he was waiting for an answer. He was not involved in anyway in the dislodgement of the interloping power. Indeed, he did not even seem to be aware of its existence.

There is no doubt that we are instructed to resist the devil and he will flee from us (James 4:7). But there is no evidence that this is a matter of verbal declaration as in a mantra. The immediate preceding instruction is to draw near to God. If drawing near to God is not expected to be done as a verbal declaration, why should the second part be necessarily executed in that fashion? In both cases it is a matter of inner spiritual attitude on the part of the praying person.

Similarly, reference is often made to the fact that Jesus said that a strong man does not take over a house unless he first binds the occupant (Matthew 12:29). But here again, it is not a matter of mantra. Nowhere in the New Testament do we hear either the Lord or His apostles verbally binding spirits. It is rather a matter of coming against them from a victorious and superior spiritual disposition.

With reference to casting out spirits, there is no question but that this was a regular practice in the New Testament. However, it was always in cases where evil spirits manifestly possessed people. In such cases, one can address the spirit authoritatively to get them to leave the possessed person.

Lest we be misunderstood, though, let us not assume that the problem here is prayer volume. Arguably, loud praying is more culturally suited to Africans than to their Chinese or Japanese brothers and sisters. Thankfully, God's ears are good enough to hear the quiet whispers coming from the Far East and he is not in any sense put off by heightened volume coming out of Africa. The problem is when we become less of suppliants and begin to act as though we ourselves are in control.

Here in Nigeria prayer as decreeing and commanding rather than as communion and humble supplication is not confined to Pentecostal churches but has become common in a wide variety of churches throughout the nation. For example, a prayer guide for the 2015 National Prophetic Prayer Conference at the Orita Mefa Baptist Church, Ibadan included prayers for unity among church leaders but also prayers *"commanding the Islamic Agenda in Nigeria and the whole world to collapse and die," "decreeing that the study of history subjects be restored to our education curriculum all over Nigeria," "decreeing that the Balogun spirits loose its hold over Christians in Nigeria," and that "whatever that kill businesses and Churches in Ibadan die by fire of God."* [85]

The sad picture here is that much too often when prayer becomes primarily characterized by commanding, decreeing, and combat, we have moved out of the context of the Bible and into something else. When we find ourselves chanting the name of Jesus and *Holy Ghost fire* almost as a talisman and engaging in attempts to command and decree things to pass, in the belief that it is the best way to break through and release the flow of God's blessings, we may no longer necessarily be talking about the faith once and for all delivered to the saints. Rather, we may well have unwittingly borrowed a chapter from the African Traditional Religion playbook, even if it is decorated with a few scriptures from the Bible.

> **REALITY CHECK:** Prayer primarily as commands and decrees and prayers addressed to Satan and demons are not what the Christian Church has experienced over the centuries. This is not the normal nature of prayer as found in the scriptures. Rather, this is prayer conditioned by African Traditional Religion mentality, where struggle with the spirit world dominates attention rather than focus on Almighty God.

Because of the importation of a truncated or tainted message received not from mainstream Pentecostalism but from its fringes we continue to struggle today with inadequate Bible interpretation given to us by leaders who have bought into the health and wealth gospel, including faulty exegesis of a

---

[85] Email received by Gary Maxey 7 December, 2015.

handful of favorite scripture passages that continue to be quoted out of context. Sound Bible teaching has become less important. A relatively small number of oft-repeated verses have become our stock-in-trade. *"We are not the tail but the head"* (Deuteronomy 28:13), *"I wish above all things that thou mayest prosper and be in health"* (3 John 2), *"Concerning the work of my hands command ye"* (Isaiah 45:11). Little or no effort is expended to properly exegete the word. Regrettably, the people respond to it with eagerness, and keep coming back for more, with the "man of God" reaping rich material rewards from the unsuspecting flock.

BLURRING THE LINES

Dennis Kinlaw and John Oswalt have spoken about the blurring of lines between biblical teaching and animistic beliefs. They note that within scriptures there is an important boundary between the divine and the human, but that this boundary is not present in animistic religions. In his *Lectures in Old Testament Theology* Kinlaw notes that it is only within Judaism, Christianity and Islam that there is an unmistakable and impassable demarcation between the realm of the divine and the non-divine (what Kaufmann labels the "metadivine").[86] However, as we have already pointed out in the previous chapter, Word of Faith theology has a lot to say about the *lack* of boundaries between God and man, and that we not only are gods ourselves but that we can through faith do what God Himself does.

Oswalt makes similar observations. Within all world religions except those based on the Bible *"everything that exists, whether human, natural, or divine, is continuous with everything else that exists.*

---

[86]Dennis Kinlaw, *Lectures in Old Testament Theology* (Anderson, Indiana: Francis Asbury Press, 2010), pp. 78-79.

. . . The character of the gods is identical with that of humans, only on a grander scale." Because God is not a part of the cosmos and has absolute power, magic and sorcery are prohibited. God cannot be manipulated, and certainly not by manipulating the cosmos.[87]

Richard Gehman further notes that within ATR,

> *Magic refers to the saying of set words and the doing of set acts in order to control and bend the powers of the world to do what a person wishes. Magic is forcing something to happen instead of praying to God for something to happen. Magic grows from the belief that the universe is filled with a power that man can use to help or harm others if only he will say and do the right things.*[88]

Because *"Faith is the substance of things hoped for and the certainty of things not seen,"*it is taught by many in the contemporary Nigerian Church that you can virtually wish anything and materialize it just by believing it. No thought is given that, above all, what is being asked for must first be in keeping with the will of God. Faith is the substance of things God has promised but which have not become real yet. Therefore, we need to first obtain a promise from God before we can exercise faith in Him in that regard. When we fast or pray all manner of prayer over something that God has not promised us, it is attempted manipulation.

If we understand these principles and distinctions clearly we will see that much of the fringe Pentecostalism imported from America has blurred and then crossed the line into something that is fundamentally neither scriptural nor safe.

---

[87]John N. Oswalt, *Called to be Holy: A Biblical Perspective* (Anderson, Indiana: Francis Asbury Press, 1999), pp. 11-14.
[88]Gehman, *Op cit,*p. 53.

FLIRTING WITH BLATANT OCCULTISM

We would not be as thorough as we should if we did not note that the revival of African Traditional Religion within the Nigerian Church involves more than just covert and ideological or conceptual concessions. There is also disturbing and reportedly growing evidences of overt occultism within the church.

Most of the stories of overt occultism within the church come as second- and third-hand reports. Many of us are inclined to take such reports as unproven hearsay and to dismiss them or at least to receive them with ample doses of skepticism. At the least we assume they could be exaggerated and embellished as they are passed on from mouth to mouth. Reports of pastors burying human skulls inside churches to obtain power, or of seeking out and consulting with witches or demonic spirits are not uncommon. At times such reports circulate in the news media as well, including both the national dailies and the religious news media.

As an example of what we are describing, Gary received a report in November 2015 entitled "Confession of a Pastor of How Pastors of Many Churches of This Generation Use Mami-Wata Powers to Perform Miracles and Wonders in their Various Churches." After reading through the report he found some of its allegations not only disturbing but also highly challenging to his more rational faculties. He wrote to a widely respected Nigerian pastor and church leader who had been copied in the same report and asked him how much credence he would advise him to give to the allegations. In his response the leader noted, *"I classify the story as charismatic witchcraft which some of us have always condemned. We do speak out on such occultism practices. . . . We need to keep up warning ministers trusting that they will listen and refrain from such practices.*"[89]

No one can say for sure how accurate such reports are or how common these things are within the Nigerian Church. Yet few doubt they are happening, and that direct engagement in ancient occult practices is ongoing and perhaps even on the rise. What sometimes makes the temptations to move in this direction particularly irresistible is that many followers with itching ears nurse a desire to have their problems solved at any cost, as Paul mentions in 2 Timothy 4:3. Such people can easily encourage leaders to go to any necessary length to acquire powers outside the one legitimate source of Christian power, which is the Holy Spirit. We must never forget that there are only two sources of power in the universe: God and Satan. In either case there is an unavoidable price that must be paid. For God it is purity, total surrender and holiness of life (1 Peter 1:15-16). And for Satan it is the eternal damnation of our soul.

Sunday Agang cites examples of witchcraft within Nigeria perpetuated by Christians against fellow church members. He cites a 2010 CNN interview of a project coordinator for Stepping Stones Ministry, which is ostensibly dedicated to helping street children. In the interview the coordinator noted,

> *Religious leaders capitalize on the ignorance of some parents in the villages just to make some money off them. They can say your child is a witch and if you bring the child to the church, we can deliver the child, but eventually they don't deliver the children... The parents go back to the pastor and say, "Why is it you have not been able to deliver the child?" and the pastor says, "Oh, this*

---

[89] This report was given in an email from Oged Orekyeh to Gary Maxey, 28 November 2015; see subsequent email from Gary Maxey to Austen Ukachi, 28 November 2015; responding email from Austen Ukachi to Gary Maxey, 22 December 2015.

one has gone past deliverance; they've eaten too much flesh so you have to throw the child out." The CNN report found that most pastors charge a fee for deliverance anywhere from $300 to $2,000."[90]

SORCERY IN THE NAME OF CHRISTIANITY

Though blatant occultism and open engagement with demonic spirits is apparently on the increase in the Nigerian Church it is not the primary evidence of the resurgence of African Traditional Religion in the country. Rather, there are dozens of other ways in which subtle ATR influences and impulses to sorcery are growing. Some of the evidences in and of themselves may seem innocuous or without serious meaning, while others are more troubling. The growing cost and elaboration of ceremonies such as funerals, burials, weddings and coronations and killing of many cows is one case in point, though not serious enough to evoke our deep concern here. Mania over taking of titles is on the rise. The pronouncing of curses, and incorporating it as a major element in prayer is stunning. Celebrating second, third and fourth burials, assuring success in heaven, is becoming more common.

It is not always easy to distinguish what is legitimate and what it not, but many familiar with global Christianity believe that the twenty-first century worldwide is experiencing a growth in occultism. Richard Gehman notes:

> *Africa is not alone in the experience of mystical powers, the unseen forces in the world we live. These beliefs have been hard to remove even in those countries where the Gospel has been*

---

[90]Sunday Bobai Agang, "The Greatest Threat to the Church Isn't Islam – It's Us," *Christianity Today*, April 21, 2017, http://www.christianitytoday.com/ct/2017/may/radical-islam-not-nigerian-churchs-greatest-threat.html. Accessed 30 April 2017.

preached for hundreds of years. Today beliefs in magic, divination, communication with the dead, spiritism, astrology and devil worship are being revived throughout the West. In fact, the belief and practice in mystical powers (the occult) is the fastest growing religion of the United States and Western Europe. [91]

The scriptures have numerous warnings about engagement with sorcery or any form of mystical powers. The longest teaching in the Bible concerning mystical powers is found in Deuteronomy 18:9-14. Seeking supernatural means to harm others is forbidden, as well as using magic to help people. According to the Bible all such mystical powers are evil and are forbidden for believers. Deuteronomy describes it as "detestable." God does not want His people to be associated with the enemies of the Kingdom of God. This is why the Bible thoroughly forbids the use of mystical powers, whether they are approved by our society or not. [92]

It is when we look at the flood of covert sorcery inundating the contemporary Nigerian Church that we become truly disturbed. What we see helps us understand a primary reason why revival tarries. Yet a major segment of the Church has had a mixed response to the sorcery and indeed finds it difficult much of the time to recognize it for what it really is or even acknowledge that it is there.

---

[91] Richard Gehman, *Op cit.*, p. 81; Halloween is the second most widely-celebrated holiday in the USA, in which even multitudes of nominal Christians celebrate occultism, largely in ignorance. Malcolm J. McVeigh notes that the global phenomenon Gehman is talking about is not absent from Africa: *"The truth of the matter is that the belief in witchcraft has not been reduced by missionary influence or contact with the West. On the contrary, it is possible to argue that belief in witchcraft has never been greater and that it is in fact growing rapidly in present-day Africa."God in Africa*, 1974, quoted by Jonathan Iorighir, "Gender and The Challenge of Witchcraft," *Living With Dignity: African Perspectives on Gender Equality*, Elna Mouton, Gertrude Kapuma, Len Hansen, Thomas Togom, eds. (Stellenbosch: SUN MeDIA, 2015), pp. 112-113.

[92] Gehman, *Op cit.*, pp. 99-101.

When it shows up in its more flamboyant forms such as in the ministry of the highly controversial T. B. Joshua, Pentecostal leaders occasionally roundly condemn it.[93] Joshua's popularity both inside and outside Nigeria is enormous. His healing ministry is nearly without parallel. His "anointing water" has been distributed far and wide with claims of power to heal all kinds of diseases, including HIV/AIDS as well as the deadly Ebola that struck Sierra Leone in 2014, and to which Joshua responded by sending 4,000 bottles of his water. Both the Christian Association of Nigeria and the Pentecostal Fellowship of Nigeria have distanced themselves from Joshua. Other prominent church leaders who have denounced him publicly have labeled him a "son of the devil."

Interestingly, however, the very practices that have made T. B. Joshua popular and that have boosted his image as a man of power and healing also show up in a wide range of other Nigerian churches. The most obvious is the exploding use of olive oil for various kinds of anointing. We could also point out the growing use of blessed handkerchiefs (or mantles) and holy water. It appears that investment in the Nigerian olive oil market would have been a very wise move twenty years ago!

Perhaps no church leader in Nigeria has garnered as much attention and criticism for his use of olive oil as Bishop David Oyedepo, head of the Living Faith Church Worldwide (aka, Winners Chapel), founder of two large private universities, and pastor of the largest congregation in metropolitan Lagos. In his 1992 book, *Anointing for Breakthrough*, Oyedepo tells of pastors who anointed their pulpits with oil that he had

---

[93]Ayo Onikoyi, "How other men of God see TB Joshua," *Vanguard*, September 27, 2014, http://www.vanguardngr.com/2014/09/men-god-see-tb-joshua/. Accessed 17 January 2017.

provided and thereby made it possible for their members to receive instant healing. He notes,

> *[The anointing oil] upgrades the authority of your tongue and makes your words effective when you speak, causing the things you declare to come to pass. . . . It has blessed thousands of people around the world today, because it is sealed by the Holy Spirit. . . . The anointing oil is not a symbol. . . . Through the medium of the anointing oil, the beneficiary can enjoy the supernatural ministry of the Holy Spirit.*[94]

In his operational manual for his churches, Bishop Oyedepo is even more explicit. There he notes the following:

> *The mystery of the anointing oil is another blessing we have seen produce such terrific, mind-blowing results in this Church. The anointing oil is not for ritual purposes, neither is it a magic wand. It is not a symbol, and its application is not for religious rites. It is not a mere chemical product, nor is it just oil. . . . It is the Spirit of God, mysteriously packaged in the oil, and designed to communicate the power of God bodily.*[95]

We would hope that with this kind of teaching few objective observers would question the fact that we have crossed a line from acceptable practice into age-old African sorcery, no matter who is advocating it. The fact that these practices "work" or produce results is not a valid test of scriptural soundness. We need to stand against these practices with a strong biblical voice. Men like Pastor Tunde Bakare, among others within the Nigerian Church, have risen to rebuke

---

[94]David Oyedepo, *Anointing for Breakthrough* (Lagos: Dominion Publishing House, 1992, 2014 reprint), pp. 177, 225 [emphasis mine].

[95]David Oyedepo, *The Mandate Operational Manual, Living Faith Church Worldwide a.k.a. Winners Chapel International*, Foreword by David O. Oyedepo, 2012, Dominion Publishing House, p. 142.

Oyedepo for teaching that *"the anointing oil is the Holy Spirit in a bottle."*[96]

Ali notes that the introduction of various kinds of sorcery into the Nigerian Church extends far beyond the use and abuse of anointing oil.

> *It has got to such an extent that some gospel preachers have now resorted to using some metaphysical concepts and spiritism to induce spiritual power they need to solve people's physical, material and social problems. In some circles, the people of God are now instructed through some special mystery revelations. Some claim, to carry "holy" water, "holy" oil, "miracle" mantle. Some mix black currant water with a drop of olive oil for the "blood of sprinkling" to ward off dangers, and conduct foot-washing services for material break-throughs. Some use direct occultic media such as charms, "power" soap and occultic rings, etc. to perform some extra ordinary acts in an attempt to meet man's temporal needs. Ironically, these non-biblical methods seem to work for them. The belief is that "if it works, it is good and if it is good, then it is God because God is good." This is a type of Joseph Fletcher situational ethics that advocates that the end justifies the means. Strangely enough a substantial amount of crowds follow these religious gurus. Pathetic![97]*

The belief that curative powers reside physically in objects that have been handled or touched or worn by leaders within the Nigerian Church has grown steadily over the past decades. For example, David Oyedepo recounts the positive healing effects his followers experienced when after preaching before a large crowd he flung his sweat-soaked suit jacket into the audience

---

[96]Victorson Agbenson, *Moment of Truth: The Compelling Story of Pastor Tunde Bakare* (Ibadan, Safari Books Ltd, 2014), pp. 262-267.
[97]Ali, *Op cit.*, p. 29

and people clamored to rub it over their bodies to absorb physical benefits for themselves.[98] In a similar manner, E. A. Adeboye tells of women clamoring at the close of a service to get onto the platform in order to sit briefly in the same chair where he had sat, so they could be physically healed or conceive - and with positive effects. One frustrated woman who could not get her turn to sit in Adeboye's chair instead managed to rub her belly on the pulpit from where he had preached, reportedly achieving her own desired pregnancy that same month.[99]

We know that in the New Testament people received objects that had touched the apostles or stood in their shadows to receive healing. However, those practices were exceptions because of the throng or because the sick people could not be physically brought to the place where the apostles were. However, we fear that the wholesale practice of such activities makes them the norm rather than the exception. That would be dangerously skirting the line of demarcation between the biblically acceptable and the excessive.

We must make it clear that we have confidence in the integrity and in the general goodness and positive influence of these two great Nigerian church leaders. We honor them for their service to God and to the Nigerian Church. However, in the context

---

[98]David Oyedepo, *Understanding the Anointing*, 1998, 2010 reprint, Dominion Publishing House, p. 137. *"When it was time to minister to the sick, God spoke to me to pass my jacket around, for a touch by anyone who desired healing. . . . the Lord instructed me to pass round the overflowing native attire (agbada) I had on. When it got to her turn, she laid it on her tummy and become pregnant that same month!"*

[99]Enoch A. Adeboye, *Come Up Higher With Prayer Points*, 2013, Printme Communications Company, Lagos, p. 179. There seems to be a very thin line between these kinds of practices and "contagious magic" practiced in African Traditional Religion. The concept of "contagious magic" is that things that have once been in contact with each other continue to act on each other at a distance, even after the physical contact has been removed. See Gehman, *Op cit*, pp. 56-57.

where for centuries ATR has taught that spiritual power lies in physical objects this kind of practice is not easy to defend. At the very least much clearer teaching is needed to distinguish that which is biblical from that which veers into ATR.

As we have suggested above, there is a great need here for more open dialogue within the Nigerian Church on these issues. We are not suggesting that there are always easy answers on where to draw the line between what is biblical and what is not. And of course the solution is never to simply import answers from overseas. The need for critical self-theologizing on the part of the Nigerian Church is clear.

Ali is not alone in raising the alarm against the rise of elements of age-old sorcery within the Nigerian Church, including things that are very akin to the practices going on long before the arrival of the Christian message. For example, Ogunkani notes,

> [There are many] new fangled methods to prosperity: . . . The use (misuse) of anointing oil to obtain God's favor in the area of prosperity is one of the most common of these weird practices. Sellers of olive oil have been doing roaring business as more and more people purchase them for anointing their foreheads, business premises, wares, and even to drink, in order to obtain the favor of God and "make it." To say the least, anointing oil was never prescribed in the Bible for such practices...But people claim that this has come as a new revelation from God, and that "it works." ...Another of these strange practices is that which involves the use of the so-called "mantle." These are handkerchiefs that have been specially "blessed." They are then held in pockets for use as nothing more than good-luck charms. As needed, they are brought out and used to wipe the face. Such practices will bring instant favors from God and man, it is claimed. . . . Some have even gone to the extent of using occult

and fetish powers to obtain results so as to attract an ever increasing number of people to themselves." [100]

> **REALITY CHECK:** Attributing spiritual powers to inanimate objects has not been the teaching of orthodox Christianity through the centuries. When the Church has veered off in that direction correctives have always risen to bring us back on track. The Bible teaches that power does not reside in objects but in Almighty God. On the other hand, African Traditional Religion has often located power in material objects — charms, talismans, etc. To defend the use of physical objects as conveyers of spiritual power on the basis that it "works" is no excuse for allowing this type of potential sorcery into the Church.

The use of magic to bring about healing is another unmistakable sign of occultism. Kinlaw observed, *"in magic there is no appeal to a personal god."* [101] Onofurho also notes that

> *When one's faith has to be placed on the minister or the person doing the healing rather than in God, it is falsehood. In divine healing, faith is not in any object but in Christ the Healer. When faith is in "holy water," "anointing oil," "mantel," etc., one is involved with sorcery (idolatry). When the minister or person doing the healing, depends on any other source for him to heal other than Jesus Christ, it is falsehood.* [102]

A final emphasis within the contemporary Nigerian Church that has taken us into questionable territory is the practice of calling down judgment and curses on those who are perceived as standing in the way of personal success or prosperity. It is not

---

[100] Ogunkanmi, *Contending*, pp. 87-88.

[101] Dennis F. Kinlaw with John N. Oswalt, *Lectures in Old Testament* Theology (Anderson, Indiana: Francis Asbury Press, 2010), p. 78.

[102] Emmanuel O. Onofurho, *Contending*, p. 54.

uncommon these days for entire congregations to be encouraged to call down the fire of God upon their flesh-and-blood enemies, even though such things were never heard of in previous Christian generations.

I (Gary) will never forget the shock I felt nearly twenty years ago when I walked into a Lagos congregation of about 5,000 people on a Sunday morning in the middle of a section where the leader was urging them to call down curses on *"whoever is preventing your promotion at work."* The crowd was in a frenzy, collectively calling down the wrath of God on real people. Frankly, I did not have to be told that I had moved out of the bounds of Bible Christianity that morning.

Practices of this sort have their ultimate roots in African Traditional Religion and not in the Holy Bible. The Bible mandate is for us to turn the other cheek (Matthew 5:39; Luke 6:29). Paul says in obviously figurative language that we are to heap burning coals on the heads of our enemies by returning good for evil. It is God who avenges evil, but we are not to take such matters into our own hands. That is the plain and repeated message of the scriptures.

Nevertheless, the Nigerian Church has gone far in our generation to teach its members to call down curses in very explicit terms. In his book, *Dynamics of Prayer*, Odinkemere offers a typical prayer:

> *Lord, it is written in Psalm 68 "let God arise, let his enemy be scattered." Therefore, my Father and my God, I ask you to arise in my family and let any household enemies be scattered. Be scattered!! Be scattered!! In the mighty name of Jesus Christ. Seven times. Father let your violent fire of judgment begin to torment them wherever they are. Seven times, in Jesus' name.*

All of this is quite contrary to the plain teaching of Jesus in places such as the Sermon on the Mount. There Jesus commands us to love our enemies, to bless those that curse us, to do good to them that hate us, and to pray for those who persecute us (Matthew 5:38-48). In like manner, Peter urges believers to overcome evil by exhibiting God's love (1 Peter 3:9). From the Bible perspective, we "destroy" our enemies by doing good to them and by making them our friends. We bless them. Romans 12:14 could not be any clearer: *"Bless those who persecute you, bless and do not curse."* Just what part of *"do not curse"* do we not understand? Our attitude as Christians is persistently redemptive, and never retaliatory. St. Augustine taught that the coals of fire heaped upon our enemies' heads are not retaliatory but rather the burning pangs of shame or anguish that lead to repentance.

We are aware that appeals to the so-called "imprecatory psalms" (Psalms 35, 52, 58, 59, 69, 109, 139) are sometimes used as justification for cursing of real or imagined enemies. But David is speaking in these psalms in his capacity as the king of Israel asking God to vindicate His cause by dealing with His enemies. These psalms are not David expressing personal vindictiveness. Rather, he is appealing to God to uphold justice and righteousness and to corporately protect His cause and His kingdom. Moreover, when we read narratives such as that found in 1 Samuel 24, we can see who David really was in his heart. There David had an easy opportunity to personally wreak vengeance and even death on the man who not only was his enemy but who was out to kill him. Yet his response was to display incredible mercy and restraint.

Like other leaders in the scriptures who spoke out against the enemies of God (Moses, in Numbers 10:55; Nehemiah, in Nehemiah 4:4-5, and Jeremiah, in Jeremiah 18:19-23) the cry is always for divine judgment and not for petty personal vindication or retaliation. All of these prophets of old knew the law of God, and among other things its prohibition against sorcery, and against the casting of spells or cursing of our enemies, as can be plainly seen in Deuteronomy 18:10-11. God's plan has always been to bless the world through His people, and that never happens when they resort to cursing others. Those who do so have moved beyond the world of the Bible and have embraced the kingdom of the enemy.

> **REALITY CHECK:** The pronouncing of curses on other people has not been the teaching of the Christian Church down through the ages. The scriptures directly forbid such practices. However, cursing of people is an integral part of African Traditional Religion.

How Serious is This Issue?

We are well aware that some of our readers may rush to defend some of the practices we have mentioned. They may allege that we are worrying too much, even though we are strongly warning that what we see here is not the religion of the Bible. Allan Anderson, a former researcher in southern Africa and senior lecturer in the Centre for Missiology and World Christianity at the University of Birmingham, England, is of the opinion that *"the fact that so many manifestations of the Spirit encountered in the Spirit churches have parallels in pre-Christian religion should not unduly alarm us."* [103] He believes the Holy Spirit has sanctified numerous religious expressions that were found earlier within ATR. However, we believe there is a crucial need for caution, lest we lose the inner meaning of what lies

---

[103] Allan Anderson, "African Initiated Churches of the Spirit and Pneumatology," *Word & World*, Volume 23, Number 2, Spring, 2003, p. 185.

under outward practices or rituals. It is not difficult for us to open the door to counterfeit spiritual manifestations, though we must also not forget that Africa does not have a monopoly on counterfeit spiritual manifestations, any more than a monopoly on syncretism.

Again, we believe the time is past due for those of us in the Nigerian Church to speak plainly to each other about these matters. We have gradually allowed African Traditional Religion to creep into our churches unchecked and unrebuked. And the truth is that the most rapidly growing churches among us are often those with the most egregious violations. We have crossed the line again and again into occult practices and into methods and philosophies that are borrowed from our African pre-Christian past. We need to sound a strong warning that this is not the religion of the Bible.

We do not intend to pronounce a totally negative verdict on African culture. We have already observed that its worldview is in many ways more compatible with that of the Bible than is the western secularized worldview. And there is no question that African Traditional Religion did much to prepare the continent for the receiving of the full revelation of God through Jesus Christ. Yet ATR falls far short of the heart of the Bible. There is very little or nothing in ATR about sin as rebellion against God or that points the way to a new birth restoration of fellowship with God. There is no offer of salvation. John Mbiti puts it this way: *"African religions and philosophy must admit a defeat: they have supplied no solution. This remains the most serious cul-de-sac in the otherwise rich thought and sensitive religious feeling of our peoples. It is perhaps here then, that we find the greatest weakness and poverty of our traditional religions."*[104]

---

[104]John S. Mbiti, *African Religions and Philosophy* (Heinemann; 2nd Revised & enlarged edition, 1990), p. 99.

We need to be clear once again that truth is not tested properly either by what "pulls crowd" or what "works." The magic of Pharaoh's magicians worked, and lying signs and wonders are as old as Satan himself. Mushrooming attendance and building of large buildings is not a measure of Bible success. Often, what we have achieved in recent years is to baptize ancient tenets of African religion with a light sprinkling of out-of-context scripture. Sadly, the end product is not the unadulterated religion of Jesus Christ.

The Bible does not teach us that we need special help from a powerful church leader to get a breakthrough. To the contrary, God is near us and ever ready to help a very present help in time of need (Psalm 46:1). Isaiah assures us God's arm is not too short nor His ear too heavy, but that only our own sins have separated us from Him (Isaiah 59:1). And the scriptures give us precise answer on how we can side with God to remove sin as a barrier in our lives. There is no need to speak to demons or ancestral spirits in order to break through to God. There is no need to chant the name of Jesus or to assume that we have the power to command or decree the solutions to our needs. It is really only our sin that can create a barrier, and Jesus has paid the price to decisively remove that barrier from our lives.

There is no doubt that God has given special spiritual gifts to some in the body of Christ to use for the benefit of others in need (Ephesians 4:9-14). However, it must be borne in mind that these people should function in such a way as to enable Christians from within the congregation to do the work of the ministry (Ephesians 4:11-12). In other words, ministry is not to be monopolized by a few gifted ministers, whether in preaching, teaching or working of miracles. That would tend to make them look like the African traditional priests who function as professional specialists upon whom the people solely and permanently depend. It is dangerous because it results in dependency and adulation. Dependency on big ministers tends to remove focus from God. Adulating them runs the risk of destroying them by turning them to demigods. Genuine success in ministry occurs when one gets others to do the same work that he does. That is when true growth takes place in the body of Christ (Ephesians 4:16).

We are not suggesting that demonic spirits are not real or that they cannot cause problems. But Jesus is the answer. He has all power or authority in heaven and on earth. The simplest child who has faith in God and has surrendered to the lordship of Jesus Christ can get into the throne room of God through prayer, without any need to break through ranks of demonic or ancestral spirits to do so. So whether the "breakthrough" being sought is the removing of obstacles for financial or other earthly success or the demolishing of real satanic strongholds, God has made it possible for every born again believer to be a daily victor.

Nor do we have to be always dependent on a great "man of God" to lay hands on us in order to receive God's blessings, though there is surely a legitimate place for the man of God and we thank God for all those he is using among us. But we always remember that Jesus Christ is our all-sufficient mediator. We recognize the biblical use of oil in healing, as advocated by the apostle James. Yet we do not need protection by water or oil that has been prayed over, or by means of any other amulet, or any white handkerchief on the doorpost or any object in the pocket in the name of a "point of contact." All of these are often little or no different from the sorcery that has been played out in Africa over past millennia.[105]

---

[105]Emmanuel O. Onofurho, *Contending*, p. 54.

Byang Kato, the energetically-rising evangelical star of African theologians whose young life was cut short forty years ago, saw even in his own day the pending revival of African Traditional Religion within the African Church. He spoke out against it in clear tones: *"The defunct gods of African traditional religions are now rearing their heads. . . . Christo-paganism appears to be the area of attack within the next generation. The battle has started."*[106] Kato could never have imagined how much the shape of the battle lines would change in forty years, but even now we are in the midst of the battle. No one can deny that we have lived to see enormous seduction of the Nigerian Church in this area.

God's answer is scriptural revival. It is a robust and rigorous return to scripture. It is the revival of personal intimacy with God and of scriptural praying. And it is thorough repentance and a return to a yearning Heavenly Father. God can and will revive his church as we faithfully turn our backs on false teaching and embrace God's truth once again. Surely there is great hope for Nigeria.

---

[106]Byang Kato, *Theological Pitfalls in Africa*, 1975, Evangel Publishing House, Nairobi, p. 173. Keith Ferdinando has confirmed Kato's legacy as *"the founding father of modern African evangelical theology,"* "The Legacy of Byang Kato," International Bulletin of Missionary Research, Vol. 28, No 4, October 2004, pp. 169-174.

REDEFINING SPIRITUALITY

Nothing we have said so far in this book touches as closely to the heart of the gospel as what we want to explore in this chapter. In Chapter Four we said the unbalanced prosperity message is truly devastating the Nigerian Church. Then in Chapter Five we suggested the infusion of practices and mentality from African Traditional Religion is equally disturbing. But nothing hits closer to the heart of Christianity than a distortion of the message of holiness. Our thesis in this chapter is that there has been a costly redefinition of spirituality in the contemporary Nigerian Church that threatens to undo fundamental Bible understandings and foundational theologies. We are talking about a misunderstanding that strikes at the heart of the Bible message.

The central message of the Bible is that of total reconciliation between God and man. It is the story of redemption, and it involves much more than salvation from eternal damnation. John Oswalt helps us get at the heart of God's revelation by summarizing the teaching of the entire Bible in four simple points:

- Fallen people come into relationship with God by an act of sheer grace(*"For by grace are you saved through faith,"* Ephesians 2:8-9).

- We come into relationship with God *so that* we can fellowship with Him, on the basis of shared character(*"Be ye holy, for I am holy,"* 1 Peter 1:15-16).

- However, we discover that we cannot achieve the character of God in our own strength. *("But Israel, which followed after the law of righteousness, hath not attained to the law of righteousness. Wherefore? Because they sought it not by faith, but as it were by the works of the law,"* Romans 9:31-32).

- It is only through the power of the Holy Spirit that we are enabled to live the Christlike life. *("Walk in the Spirit, and you shall not fulfill the lust of the flesh,"* Galatians 5:16).[107]

What Oswalt is saying is that the ultimate object of God's great plan of salvation is that we should be His holy people, in intimate fellowship with a holy God for time and for eternity. Therefore, God has always sought for a holy people and has ensured that it is a practical possibility. As scripture plainly tells us, it is precisely that for which Christ died — *"Therefore Jesus also, that He might sanctify [i.e., make holy] the people with His own blood, suffered outside the gate"* (Hebrews 13:12). *"[Jesus] gave Himself for us, that He might redeem us from every lawless deed and purify for Himself His own special people, zealous for good works"* (Titus 2:14).

Because of this grand and exciting objective of God, it is the work of the Holy Spirit to purify the heart and to present us faultless before God. The psalmist declared that those who

---

[107]John Oswalt, *Called to be Holy* (Anderson, IN: Warner Press, 1999), p. 104.

will ascend into the hill of the Lord are those with *"clean hands and a pure heart"* (Psalm 24:3-4). Peter said of the work of the Holy Spirit at Pentecost that he *"purified their hearts by faith"* (Acts 15:8-9). Therefore, to be filled with the Holy Spirit means that we are His holy and Christlike people brought about through the cleansing and purifying of the heart. We must never forget that Christianity without a clear focus on holiness is not adequately biblical.

One of the consequences of this important Bible teaching is that being "filled with the Holy Spirit" has had a generally clear meaning historically within the Christian Church. A "Spirit filled" person has been primarily defined as one who is pure in heart, who lives a Christlike life, and who walks in the power of the Holy Spirit. It has pointed not primarily to outward signs and wonders but to inner character and to a reputation of holiness that is visible both privately and in public. The ensuing power, whether exercised quietly or with great demonstration, is always a concomitant to purity of heart, and never the central focus. Throughout the centuries, Spirit filled people have been most basically looked up to as exemplars of Christian ethics and personal holiness. They may well have been endowed now and again with extraordinary power, but that power has always been secondary in nature and has been defined or understood from a primary base of purity and holiness.

However, anyone familiar with the Nigerian Church today would know that this definition of "Spirit filled" has largely given way to a definition of spirituality that is not in line with the antecedents found in the past. Regrettably, the definitions have gradually become blurred. As a result, nowadays when we call someone "Spirit filled" in Nigeria we do not necessarily mean that they live like Jesus. They may in fact be living privately – and sometimes even publicly – in a manner quite contrary to Christian morality. They may be acclaimed as great "Spirit filled" men or women but may be lacking in basic areas of ethical behavior and exemplary moral living.

Frankly, this shift in meaning is not entirely new within the Nigerian Church and in fact goes back at least 100 years to the emergence of the first prophetic-healing churches. Historians such as Ogbu Kalu see a close continuity between several Nigerian Church movements that have emerged over the past century. This has led to his reference to the emergence of the neo-Pentecostal movement from the early 1970s onward as the "third response" to the cultural and religious domination of the earliest expatriate Christian missionaries of the nineteenth century. The first response was "Ethiopianism" starting in the 1880s with the emergence of the first truly African-led Christian churches. The second response was the rise of the Aladura or Zionist churches (often referred to as the prophetic-healing movement) starting in the 1920s and especially after the great Oke Oye revival in 1930.[108]

One of the linkages between all three of these responses was focus on the Holy Spirit. This is why the Aladura or prophetic-healing churches were often referred to as "spiritual" churches. Their focus was largely on the outward manifestations of Holy Spirit power (visions, prophesies, healing, etc.), but with relatively less focus on sanctification or moral holiness.

Because of this, what we refer to in this chapter could well be thought of as the "aladurization" of spirituality. Through a subtle shift from a center in personal morality and holiness to a

---

[108]Ogbu U. Kalu, "The Third Response: Pentecostalism and the Reconstruction of Christian Experience in Africa, 1970-1995," *Journal of African Christian Thought*, 1:2, 1998, p. 3.

center in outward signs of power and healing and miracles the Bible concept of holiness or spirituality was gradually muted and the measure of spirituality was significantly changed. A "Spirit filled" person was no longer necessarily an exemplar of holy living or Christlikeness in character.

It is important to also acknowledge that within the significantly secularized Western Christianity that was brought to Nigeria in the nineteenth century the concept of spirituality was too often divorced from proper understanding of the spirit world. Among many of the early Western missionaries there was also a poor understanding of the African felt need for power to confront the threats of life and triumph over them. As we have noted, the tendency of Africans was to think more holistically about the bonds between what is physical and what is spiritual. Yet the Achilles heel of the African view was a faulty concept of sin and an inadequate understanding of the all-important biblical teaching about holiness and its attendant morality. While there are clear parallels between Old Testament leaders and concepts of African leadership, exemplary leadership in the scriptures was never divorced from a high focus on ethical holiness.

In looking at spirituality within the African Independent Churches (AICs), Anderson has made the following relevant note:

> *The sine qua non of Pentecostal and "spiritual" AICs is the power of the Spirit. He is the one to whom credit is given for almost everything that takes place in church activities. Pobee and Ositelu place first in their list of "main characteristics" of AICs, "their emphasis on receiving a conscious experience of the Holy Spirit". The Spirit causes people to "receive" power, to prophesy, speak in tongues, heal, exorcize demons, have visions*

> *and dreams, and live "holy" lives – generally he directs the life*
> *and worship of the church.*[109]

The problem, however, which may indeed be indirectly indicated by Anderson placing the word holy in quote marks, is that the concept of power gradually has become less and less about moral character and more and more about power to *do* or *experience* the right things.

What we see here is a subtle shift away from the biblical concept of sin and moving in the direction of the ATR concept of sin. Within ATR sin is not understood as offense against the person and character of a holy God but rather more of social offense offending the unity or tranquility of ones community or of individuals within that community. So what we are seeing here is a valid attempt to contextualize Christianity in Africa, but apparently at the expense of biblical foundations. Anderson admits that Pentecostalism in its African expressions, like Christianity everywhere, is inherently "syncretistic".[110]

I (Gary) have pointed out elsewhere the pain that was experienced in the ministry of the younger Sydney Elton when in the '30s and early '40s he discovered that a good number of the prophets who were at the forefront of the revival that emanated from Oke Oye were living quite unChristlike and shameful lives. He was discovering that the shift from a definition of morality-based spirituality to signs-

---

[109] Anderson, *Op cit*, pp. 224-225. Anderson provides much more detail in *Moya: The Holy Spirit in an African Context* (Pretoria: University of South Africa Press, 1991), and "African Initiated Churches of the Spirit and Pneumatology," *Word & World*, Volume 23, Number 2, Spring 2003.

[110] Anderson, *African Reformation: African Initiated Christianity in the 20th Century*, Africa World Press Inc., Trenton, NJ, 2001, p. 182.

and-wonders based spirituality had already begun.[111] What seems clear is that over the decades there has been a primary shift from a focus on *character and morality* to *experience and practice*. It is a difference between what people *are* and what people *do*. It is an attempt at a total definition change regarding the concept of biblical holiness. The consequences are enormous.

It is highly lamentable that we have reached a stage in the contemporary Nigerian Church where it is possible for men of God in leadership (and sometimes women) to become guilty of serious sins that over the years have been considered serious enough to warrant dismissal from the ministry and yet continue on in ministry without serious rebuke or discipline. They can continue to display all of the outward signs of "spirituality" even while engaged in untoward behavior. We should be clear in our understanding that such people are not spiritual or "Spirit filled" in any Bible sense, no matter how impressive their spiritual gifts may be. All of their apparent spiritual gifts notwithstanding, such people are not true prophets or people of God as defined in the scriptures. At times is it just too easy to forget that while Satan and his demons have the capacity to counterfeit virtually all kinds of signs and wonders they do not know how to counterfeit purity of heart and Christlike character.

---

[111] Gary S. Maxey, *Capturing a Lost Vision: Can Nigeria's Greatest Revival Live Again?* (Lagos: WATS Publications, 2016), p. 221-222.

> **REALITY CHECK:** Historically within the Christian Church a "Spirit filled" person is a person who above everything else exemplifies Christlike living and holiness in character, and who also walks in the power of God. The Bible equates the filling of the Spirit with the purifying of the heart and the receiving of power for service. On the other hand, identifying unChristlike "Spirit filled" people primarily as those who perform outward signs and wonders or who display presumed spiritual gifts is not authentic Christianity.

The parade of substitutes for holiness and godly living within the contemporary church is a long one. Those who have found it challenging to deny the flesh and pursue after godliness of life and character have followed a thousand distracting substitutes. But those substitutes need to be rejected in favor of a return to the foundations of holy living.

The modern Pentecostal movement deserves much credit for bringing into focus the importance of the gifts of the Spirit. Those gifts have clearly been far too neglected by much of the historic Christian Church. It is one of the reasons Pentecostalism has grown so dramatically in places such as Nigeria. Whether we define those gifts narrowly as the nine gifts mentioned in 1 Corinthians 12, or to include additional gifts mentioned in Romans 12, Ephesians 4 or 1 Peter 4, the Pentecostal movement has reminded us that spiritual gifts are both a New Testament reality and that they are also alive and well within the Church today.

Yet we must be honest to admit that the proliferation of presumed displays of spiritual gifts within the contemporary Church has at times been accompanied by clear evidences of lack of Christian grace, Christian character and Christlike living. People of faulty character and in some cases who indulge in gross immorality and greed are at times at the forefront of those displaying apparent spiritual gifts and wielding displays of supposed spiritual power. The result has been oft-repeated cries that having now mastered the issue of spiritual gifts we need to refocus our attention on the *fruit* of the Spirit.

However, it is easy to forget that the absence of the fruit of the Spirit is a sure indicator that we are out of harmony, out of fellowship and out of character with Jesus. No amount of so-called spiritual gifts is compatible with unChrist like character. In fact, the operation of any so-called spiritual gift within the life of one not living like Jesus is more than likely the display of a false gift and should be regarded as such.

One of the by-products of our redefinition of spirituality within the Nigerian Church is the rise of leadership marked not by godly maturity but by outward signs and wonders and in some cases by the sheer lure of personal flamboyance and mesmerizing rhetoric. This is particularly true when combined with the attraction of money and material success displayed by the leader and promised to the followers who will follow his teachings and instructions. It is assumed by all too many that these "men of God" who promise to help people "make it," or to "break through" and who play the part by displays of their own personal material prosperity are the ones to follow.

This syndrome is in many instances the reaping of the harvest from decades of conditioning by a continual search for the spectacular. Wherever there is a downplaying of the doctrine and teaching of holiness and sanctification it becomes easy to begin to redefine spirituality. Sydney Elton noted early on in his magazine, *Herald of the Last Days:"The Holy Spirit is moving again and the gifts are being restored with the increase of signs and wonders and the demonstration of the miraculous, as experienced in the early church.*"[112] However, all of this came at a time when there was a notable decline in emphasis on holiness and sanctification. It is no wonder that the definition of spirituality got lost in the process.

It is regrettable that all across Nigeria this type of leadership continues to rise in seemingly unstoppable waves. Pastor Tunde Bakare has cried out against the rise of what he calls the "yuppie pastor" syndrome. It not only fits the description we have just given but is a clear by-product of the redefinition of spirituality about which I am talking:

> *Look at the yuppies! I went to Port Harcourt to minister and we were going to the hotel and I saw a church there. When I saw the skimpy skirts and all kinds of things, my heart was grieved and I said, "God have mercy." These are babies pastoring babies. They are now called at eighteen; by nineteen they have launched their international ministry; before they are twenty, they are already buying a jeep; by the time they are twenty-five, they need an armored car and armored tanks to protect them robbers and bastards on the pulpit, untaught, uncooked and unpolished. No man had a significant ministry in Israel until thirty.*

> *Yes, God can call you earlier, he even knew Jeremiah before he was conceived in his mother's womb. You can be anointed before you are that age, but you are not appointed yet, you are an arrow kept in the quiver, waiting for the time you will be shot out. When you allow men to shoot you out before your time, you miss the target, you dwell in iniquity, and you fall short of God's*

---

[112]Sydney Elton, "God's True Church in Nigeria," *Herald of the Last Days*, No. 6, p. 11, quoted in Ayodeji Abodunde, *Messenger: Sydney Elton and the Making of Pentecostalism in Nigeria* (Lagos, PierceWatershed, 2016) p. 191.

> *glory. God is not a mission in a hurry. . . . Yuppie pastor, go and sit down!*[113]

What is clear here is that with the rise of this new kind of leadership within the Nigerian Church the earlier definitions of spirituality are all but forgotten. The focus has gradually shifted away from morality and Christlike character and is now tilted much more in the direction of materialism, personal success and worldly prosperity.

Allan Anderson provides some of the historic background for this in his book *Spreading Fires*.[114] He points out the fact that the entrance of Pentecostalism into the African melting pot had the effect of stimulating new and more radically transforming forms of independent churches. Those churches were often referred to as "spiritual" churches, largely because of their emphasis on the power of the Holy Spirit, including healing, prophecy and speaking in tongues. They carried with them an inherent temptation to shift the focus toward a definition of personal spirituality in terms of the display of gifts and powers rather than a definition pointing toward holiness as morality and character.

The tracing of the history behind this in West Africa would require a careful look at emerging models of native Christian leadership in Africa starting with Liberia's William Wade Harris (1860-1929), and including Nigeria's Garrick Sokari Braide (1882-1918) and Joseph Babalola (1904-1959). All three of these African "prophets" gained massive followings among people who were on the marginal fringes of Christianity and who at best were superficially engaged with

---

[113]Tunde Bakare, quote in Agbenson, *Moment of Truth*, p. 179.

[114]Allan Anderson, *Spreading Fires: The Missionary Nature of Early Pentecostalism* (Maryknoll, NY: Orbis Books, 2007, pp. 162-167.

the biblical worldview. They apparently knew relatively little about biblical standards of holiness or about what it meant to be sanctified people. The attraction of the prophets therefore was not nearly so much in their exemplifying of Christian holiness as in their power encounter with the surrounding threatening forces of evil.

William Wade Harris focused on healing and the rejection of fetishes and other practices of ATR and was reputed to have baptized up to 120,000 converts in a single year, bringing entire villages into his fold in a single day. He is regarded as the father of Christianity in Ivory Coast. To imagine that among his converts there was any appreciable understanding of Bible holiness is difficult. Even to label Harris Pentecostal would be anachronistic, but it was clear that his primary identity was as a wielder of spiritual power in the name of the God of the Bible. His church connections were most clearly with the Methodists and the Catholics and his influence was magnetic for people caught up in poverty, fear and powerlessness.

Garrick Braide, by contrast, was a highly popular Anglican revivalist in the Niger Delta. He remained within the Anglican fold until his death, even though while he was in prison in 1916 some 43,000 of his followers formed the Christ Army Church, sometimes referred to as the first "spiritual church" in Nigeria. Braide died prematurely in 1918, in the same year the Aladura movement began to emerge further west. Eventually the Apostolic Church emerged and gained force especially after the remarkable revival in 1930 under Joseph Babalola. We cannot deny the fact that eventually the emerging Aladura movement fundamentally changed the face of West African Christianity. But our primary point here is that all three of these strategic early indigenous Christian prophets Harris, Braide and Babalola represented a middle position between what we might call the "signs-and-wonders" spirituality inherited from African Traditional Religion and the biblical spirituality focused primarily on holiness of heart and life and leading to lives of spiritual power.

Today we apparently have no one with us in West Africa who could be closely compared to the William Harrises, the Garrick Braides, or the Joseph Babalolas of the past. In their place, however, we have a growing number of leaders among whom much too often there are those marked and revered more for expressions of spiritual power than for exemplary moral lives.

RECAPTURING THE BIBLICAL MESSAGE OF HOLINESS

We do not have space in this book to give a full exposition of the Bible message of holiness, but getting that message correctly will go a long way to clear up the confusion over what is and what is not spiritual in the Bible sense. We strongly believe that the revival earnestly needed by the Nigerian Church must include a balanced message in this area. The primary reason why the Nigerian Church has been seduced by the subtle redefinition of spirituality is that the quest for scriptural holiness has been largely confused and lost. Our conviction is that it can and it must be regained.

We lament the fact that the very concept of holiness has gotten a bad name in many Nigerian circles and has become equated in too many minds merely with outward displays of legalism. Holiness is therefore both misunderstood and caricatured. To listen to some of those in Nigeria who espouse holiness gives the impression that holiness is either some kind of extreme self-effort or the dogged following of strict ethical and moral standards. Both of those ideas are far from the biblical truth. Holiness is sometimes perceived as something for an elite group who have denied themselves of any possible pleasure and who have consigned themselves to a lifetime of dour asceticism. Needless to say, very few are signing up for that kind of mis-labeled "holiness."

There are three things essential to robust biblical holiness. First is a clear understanding of the goal of holiness. Second is an understanding of what it actually looks like. And third is exactly how scriptural holiness can be realized in the practical world of modern Nigeria.

Biblical holiness has everything to do with spirituality, which is the topic of this chapter. To be spiritual is to be in sync with the Holy Spirit. The reason is that God is the very embodiment of holiness. As we noted at the beginning of this chapter, John Oswalt underscores the fact that the very purpose of our existence as human beings is that we should walk in fellowship with God *on the basis of shared character*. Amos raises the rhetorical question, *"Can two walk together, unless they are agreed?"* (Amos 3:3). That is why God repeats in both testaments, with great emphasis, *"Be holy, because I am holy"* (Leviticus 19:1-2; 1 Peter 1:15-16). The very purpose of our creation is fulfilled when we walk in fellowship with God as His saints (His holy ones, or sanctified ones).

When we understand this goal we know that holiness is neither a side issue nor is it reserved for an elite group of Christians who want to do better than the average Christians around them. Nor is it a matter of following legalistic rules. Rather, it is the very purpose of God in every life. Here is how Zacharias expressed it after the birth of his son, John the Baptist:

The oath which He swore to our father Abraham: to grant us that we, being delivered from the hand of our enemies, might serve Him without fear, in holiness and righteousness before Him all the days of our life. (Luke 1:73-75).

The burning vision of Jesus Christ for His Church is that it would be a truly sanctified church, filled with men and women walking in obedience to God, who have been purified in heart, and who are truly Christlike in their personal lives, in their marriages, in their families, in their churches, in their work, in their school, and in their community. Such kingdom-oriented people are the ones who are not only ready for heaven but who are fully equipped to do exploits for Jesus in the power of the Holy Spirit here and now.

This is why Jesus died! *"Therefore, Jesus also, that He might sanctify [make holy] the people with His own blood, suffered outside the gate"* (Hebrews 13:12). Paul describes it this way:

Christ also loved the church and gave Himself for her, that He might sanctify and cleanse her with the washing of water by the word, that He might present her to Himself a glorious church, not having spot or wrinkle or any such thing, but that she should be holy and without blemish. (Ephesians 5:25-27).

That is the goal of holiness, but what does this holiness look like in practical terms? Is it men and women with somber garb and poker faces unable to laugh or kick up their heels and have fun? Is it the careful following of strict rules and regulations? If not, what is it?

Holiness in practical terms is being a true disciple of Jesus. It is sharing the joy of living like Jesus (1 Peter 2:21-24). It is living out the normal life that comes when our sins are forgiven and we are walking onward from there in a life of obedience to God and robust growth in grace. The scripture says that the *"the path of the just is like the shining sun, that shines ever brighter unto the perfect day"* (Proverbs 4:18). We are talking about a life of living fellowship with Jesus, sustained joy in the Holy Spirit (sometimes even in the midst of trials and difficulties), and steady growth in grace. It is the privilege of having a foretaste of heaven by walking in daily fellowship with God, as preparation for an eternity of excitement and joy and unbroken fellowship with God and with the redeemed of all ages. And it is being eminently equipped and empowered for service in kingdom assignments for God right where we are here on earth.

The third question for us is how this holiness is achieved here and now. What is the pathway to a life of holy living? Here is where the contemporary Nigerian Church has found itself almost universally without a clear vision. For many of them holiness of heart and life is considered literally a utopian dream. On the contrary, it is assumed and taught that practical Christian life is one of spiritual dullness and deadness. In the meantime, we much too often excuse sin in our lives by telling ourselves and others "no one is perfect." In short, we live quite far below our privileges as saints of God.

God has mapped out for us in the Holy Scriptures a solid pathway to victorious Christian living as sanctified men and women of God. He not only desires to have a holy people but He has made it eminently possible. When He commands us to be holy because He is holy it is not a cruel taunt concerning something impossible to achieve. Rather, it is His gracious invitation to enter into a life of holy living. The pathway is clear.

First, the call to holiness begins with full surrender to God in the miracle of the new birth. *"Ye must be born again"* is the foundation of the life of holiness, and the first step in that direction. Paul wrote to the Corinthians about their experience of being sanctified, or made holy, by the "washing of regeneration" (1 Corinthians 1:2; 6:11). Their life of holiness was launched right from the first day when they were born again. To be a forgiven and born again child of God is to have begun the great journey of holiness. That is why Paul addresses believers as "saints," which literally means "holy ones." Every born again child of God has already experienced the beginning of the life of holiness.

However, part of the problem in the contemporary Nigerian Church is that the new birth has become an almost meaningless term. Our churches are often nearly filled up with people who say they are born again but who know nothing of new birth as taught in the Bible. Too often it means little more than the pasting of a label over unrepentant and unchanged lives, or some kind of blanket acceptance by the Church.

In the scriptures new birth refers to a radical change of life preceded by thoroughgoing renunciation of sin, the flesh and the devil and followed by robust new life in Christ. That new life is marked by a clean conscience, by clear communion with God, and by a default lifestyle of obedience to God's will. Such are the people who are not only ready for heaven but prepared to do the good works here and now that God prepared in advance for them to do (Ephesians 2:10).

Second, the life of holiness involves growth in grace after the new birth, or what may be properly called *progressive sanctification*. This broad scope of progressive sanctification is referred to in verses such as 2 Thessalonians 2:13, where Paul notes *"God from the beginning chose you for salvation through sanctification by the Spirit and belief in the truth."* Our salvation involves the ongoing guidance, admonitions, rebukes, corrections, and comfort of the Holy Spirit. In that walk we progressively learn how to more quickly overcome temptations, more quickly obey the promptings of the Holy Spirit and more effectively serve God reflecting the spirit of Jesus Christ. Saints of God who have walked in a life of steady obedience to God for ten or twenty years are visibly more mature and more Christlike than when they first started their journey. It is because they are experiencing progressive sanctification.

Third, the pathway of holiness involves deeper dealings of the Holy Spirit regarding what the scriptures call the carnal mind (Romans 6:6), or the double mind (James 1:8). This aspect of the life of holiness is extremely important but often overlooked or even denied. Yet the reality is that there is a universal experience among those who have walked with the Lord for a period of time after their new birth. For those who continue to walk in obedience there is a shared experience of sooner or later discovering that there is a deeper spiritual need in their lives that eventually they cannot ignore. That deeper need revolves around the war within them between the spirit of Christ and the inherited sin nature that is constantly pulling them back. Sooner or later, deep within their hearts, they come face-to-face with the disturbing reality of the unconquered double mind.

It is at that point that the Holy Spirit desires to lead earnest believers to a deeper cleansing than they received at the new birth. He will also often guide them into a much deeper consecration than they experienced at the time of their new birth. But before that deeper consecration and cleansing can take place the Holy Spirit shines a strong light on the characteristics of inherited depravity that yet remain in the carnal heart. This illumination of the Spirit reveals things such as carnal anger, jealousy, love of money, and carnal pride. This is the wood, hay and stubble that God wants to burn up in the life of the believer (1 Corinthians 3:12; 2 Timothy 2:20-22). It is the filthiness of flesh and spirit Paul refers to in 2 Corinthians 7:1 and which God desires to cleanse.

What born again believer would not want to be freed from these worldly and carnal tendencies within them? Every sincere believer wants to be like Christ. The Holy Spirit cries out against the sin, the wrong temper, the pride, the lust, and the selfishness that yet lies within the heart of the double-minded believer. It is with a pure heart that we are fully prepared to enter heaven (Psalm 24:3-4), and it is the work of the Holy Spirit to bring about the illumination and the purification that will make that possible in the here and now (Acts 15:8-9).

Preaching that focuses on the need for a pure heart and for deliverance from the double mind or the carnal nature is rare these days. We naturally recoil from the negativity of focusing on the impurity within us. The body of sin resists destruction (Romans 6:6). Yet it is as the believer fully acknowledges and confesses his impurity and then yields to the Holy Spirit in a deeper consecration that he can receive the purifying fire of God applied to his needy heart.

Over and over again the scriptures promise this purification. Ezekiel talks about it: *"Then I will sprinkle clean water on you, and you shall be clean; I will cleanse you from all your filthiness and from all your idols. I will give you a new heart and put a new spirit within you"* (Ezekiel 36:25-26). Paul says, *"Having been set free from sin, you became slaves of righteousness"* (Romans 6:18). And John says, *"If we walk in the light as He is in the light, we have fellowship with one another, and the blood of Jesus Christ His Son cleanses us from all sin"* (1 John 1:7).

This deliverance from the power and presence of the carnal mind is possible, and it is part of the ongoing sanctification of the believer. Jesus died to cleanse us from all sin. This is a vital part of the "perfecting of the saints" (Ephesians 4:12). Yet we fear that believers who submit to this work of the Holy Spirit in their lives may be few and far between. Yet it is these alone who experience the deeper consecration and the deeper cleansing of the Holy Spirit that leads to a life of profoundly satisfying holiness.

It was with this very burden that Paul prayed his prayer over the Thessalonian believers:

> *Now may the God of peace Himself sanctify you completely; and may your whole spirit, soul, and body be preserved blameless at the coming of our Lord Jesus Christ. He who calls you is faithful, who also will do it.*

The terminology we use to describe these experiences is not what is most important. Just as the terminology of new birth has become confused in the contemporary Nigerian Church so, too, has the terminology of sanctification and of the baptism with the Holy Spirit. Some say that the baptism with the Holy Spirit takes place at the new birth; others say it is in a second experience of heart cleansing in the lives of believers; and yet others say that it is a third experience bringing about power. Some say it is accompanied by evidence of speaking in tongues, and others deny that. None of those are issues we can focus on here, nor do we believe they should rightfully divide us as believers.

What is most important, we believe, is that the Holy Spirit be allowed to operate fully in the lives of all believers, bringing them to a place of total surrender to God, cleansing them from every taint of the carnal nature, filling them with the fullness of the Spirit, and setting them ablaze for God and visibly filled with power for holy exploits in a life of true holiness. Such are the people that God is calling forth in Nigeria to lead the Church into a new era of revival and kingdom triumph!

THE HYPER GRACE
CHALLENGE

In the last three chapters we have laid out a case describing three general sources of the seduction of the Nigerian Church. But we cannot rest our case without discussing an additional and relatively newer threat that has arisen within the last ten-plus years and that is often referred to as the teaching of hyper grace. It is a teaching that has taken certain segments of the Nigerian Church by storm, and that has a surface attraction explaining why it has achieved such wide publicity in a relatively short period of time.

None of the deceptive teachings that have led the Nigerian Church astray over the past forty years have come to us without significant elements of truth. All of them have appealed to deeply felt needs within the hearts of hungry and thirsty Nigerians. Therefore, multitudes defend those deceptive teachings because they see them as scripturally sound. They often have personal stories of how the teachings have achieved positive effects in their lives. These things are also true for the hyper grace teaching we are examining in this chapter.

Hyper grace teaching is particularly attractive to people who have labored under a false sense of guilt inspired by heavy dosages of legalistic thinking and teaching. Both the older Pentecostal churches and the holiness movement in general have been heavily plagued by legalism over the decades. Regrettably it is much too often still the case in many of our Nigerian churches. Too many are like the Pharisees whose habit, according to Jesus, was to *"bind heavy burdens, hard to bear, and lay them on men's shoulders"* (Matthew 23:4).

None of our churches deliberately teach a doctrine of works righteousness. Nevertheless, there are probably millions of Nigerian believers who harbor open or secret doubts about their salvation because they believe they are not performing up to God's standard as they should. This is a principal telltale sign of legalism. In most cases it is because they have a faulty concept of God's grace. This is why such people are often emotionally and spiritually liberated when they hear the message of hyper grace, whether it is balanced Bible teaching or not. The problem, however, is that it is in fact *not* balanced and is a prime example of the age-old temptation and error of swinging from one doctrinal extreme to another.

The doctrine of grace is one of the most fundamental teachings of the Bible. Its importance can hardly be exaggerated. Yet any truth pressed too far becomes heresy. As the term hyper grace implies, this teaching involves an over-emphasis on grace, often to the exclusion or serious downplaying of important Bible doctrines such as repentance, confession of sin, hell and judgment.[115] We are told by those in this new movement that believers should never confess their

---

[115]Joseph Prince, for example, says that the preaching of repentance is wrong: *". . . there are still people who insist that we have to preach on repentance. Well, I disagree!"* *Unmerited Favor* (Lake Mary, FL: Charisma House, 2010), p. 232. This is obviously totally contrary to the teaching of Peter (Acts 3:19), Paul (Acts 17:30; 20:20-22; 26:19-20), and John (Revelation 2:16, 21-22; 3:3, 19).

sins, since all sins, past, present, and future, have already been forgiven. When God looks at us he sees us as holy and righteous, no matter how we may actually be living.

Furthermore, these hyper grace teachers tell us, we are not bound by the teachings of Jesus because we are not under the Old Testament law, which was still in effect until the death and resurrection of Jesus. Since all of Jesus' teachings were prior to Calvary they were still reflective of the Old Testament dispensation. Therefore, teachings of Jesus such as those in the Sermon on the Mount do not apply to Christians today.

The resulting message of hyper freedom and hyper grace is a modern form of antinomianism, *"perverting the grace of our God into a license for immorality"* (Jude 4). "Antinomianism" comes from Greek roots meaning lawlessness. An antinomian is someone who believes that under the gospel dispensation the moral law is no longer relevant because salvation is obtained through faith alone (*sola fide*). However, James' warning is quite clear, that *"faith by itself, if it does not have works, is dead"* (James 2:17, 26). So what the proponents of this new "grace revolution" or "grace reformation" are advocating is nothing but a revival of the much older heresy of antinomianism, which goes all the way back to Bible times.[116]

We are not by any means suggesting that all contemporary adherents to hyper grace in Nigeria are living wantonly

---

[116]For a summary of the errors of hyper grace see David Kowalski, "The Modern 'Grace Message' Revolution or Rebellion?,http://www.apologeticsindex.org/4981-antinomianism, accessed 10_January2017; Vic Reasoner, "Counterfeit Grace," The Arminian Magazine, Issue 1-2, Spring & Fall 2015, Vol. 33; a longer and typically irenic study is Michael L. Brown, *Hyper Grace: Exposing the Dangers of the Modern Grace Message*, (Lake Mary, FL: Charisma House, 2014), 284pp. Leaders at the forefront of the hyper grace teaching include Joseph Prince, Steve McVey, Rob Rufus, Paul Ellis, Andrew Wommack, John Crowder, Andre van der Merwe, Tullian Tchividjian, Andre Rabe, Andrew Farley and Clark Whitten.

rebellious lives and flaunting unrestrained sin. Far from it. While there are inevitably many who are attracted to this teaching as a means of assuaging their legitimate guilt over disobedience to God, others live exemplary lives despite their teaching. Nevertheless, J. Lee Grady, in his "Fire in My Bones" column in *Charisma* magazine, had this to say:

> *During a recent trip to Uganda, friends there told me of a growing church in the capital of Kampala that has been infected by the most serious form of American-style "hypergrace" teaching. The church attracts hundreds of young people who like the idea that they can fornicate whenever they want and still be right with God.*[117]

Grady went on to outline four lies that are common today among those who are spreading false doctrines. These included the idea that we do not have to repent of our sins, that we can live however we want to live sexually, that we can buy God's blessings (*"the prosperity gospel that emerged in the 1980s almost ruined our witness,"* he notes), and that God never calls us to suffer.

Even among advocates of hyper grace who are not wantonly seeking a license to sin there are serious problems. Their false doctrinal conviction that mental assent alone is sufficient for salvation has filled Nigerian churches with thousands of unrepentant and unconverted people with a false assurance of salvation. By misinterpreting the Bible message of repentance as mere mental consent rather than godly sorrow for sin they bypass one of the most important teachings of scripture.[118]

---

[117]J. Lee Grady, "Beware of Doctrines That Tickle Your Ears," *Charisma*, July 2016, p. 70.

[118]Joseph Prince, for example, in a typically pseudo-scholarly appeal to an abridged edition of Thayer's Greek lexicon, makes this mistake. David Kowalski, "A Brief Overview of the Teachings of Joseph Prince," http://www.apologeticsindex.org/3115-joseph-prince, accessed 10 January 2017.

It is to be feared that many such people are still living in subtle rebellion against God. They tend to be oblivious to God's moral authority over the redeemed. Daniel Steele, over 100 years ago, described the belief of Antinomians in this way:

A believer is not bound to mourn for sin, because it was pardoned before it was committed, and pardoned sin is no sin; that God does not see sin in believers, however great sins they commit. That by God's laying our iniquities upon Christ, He became as sinful as I, and I as righteous as Christ. Moreover, . . . no sin can do a believer any ultimate harm. [119]

REALITY CHECK: Teaching the false doctrine that believers under grace have no solemn obligation to live holy and Christlike lives is as old as the Bible itself. Our righteousness is not of our own making, but through the enablement of the Holy Spirit. Yet without it we cannot claim to be God's children. Only the righteous will inherit the kingdom of God, and righteousness is as righteousness does (*"He who practices righteousness is righteous, just as He is righteous"* [1 John 3:7]).

There is really nothing new about this teaching, even though it comes in new and attractive packaging. It involves the repetition of ancient heresies. Yet ithas nevertheless been swallowed by an amazing number of unsuspecting Nigerian churches and leaders. The Bible is quite clear that repentance is important and that there is never a point in our lives when falling into sin should not immediately call for thoroughgoing repentance, even if we are walking with the Lord as His beloved children. Jesus said to the children of God at Ephesus, *"Consider how far you have fallen! Repent and do the things you did at*

---

[119] Daniel Steele, *A Substitute for Holiness; or, Antinomianism Revived*, (Eugene, Oregon: WIPF & Stock, 2016), previously published by McDonald, Gill & Co, 1889, p. 35.

first. If you do not repent, I will come to you and remove your lampstand from its place" (Revelation 2:4). In fact, in His message to the seven churches Jesus rebukes five of them and demands repentance from them (Revelation 2:4, 6, 20; 3:3, 1519). They are quite clearly accountable for their sin, and it is also clear that they must repent if they are to continue walking with God.

The fact that this false teaching is as old as the Bible itself is made clear by John's first epistle. Already in his own day there was false teaching of antinomian Gnostics making the rounds. Gnostics taught that they had some kind of special, elite, knowledge that the masses did not know. They claimed a deeper knowledge of God that did not necessarily come from scriptures. But see how John responded to them:

> *Now by this we know that we know Him, if we keep His commandments. He who says, "I know Him," and does not keep His commandments, is a liar, and the truth is not in him. But whoever keeps His word, truly the love of God is perfected in him. By this we know that we are in Him. He who says he abides in Him ought himself also to walk just as He walked (1 John 2:3-6).*

> *These things I have written to you concerning those who try to deceive you. . . . If you know that He is righteous, you know that everyone who practices righteousness is born of Him (1 John 2:26, 29).*

> *Whoever commits sin also commits lawlessness, and sin is lawlessness. And you know that He was manifested to take away our sins, and in Him there is no sin. Whoever abides in Him does not sin. Whoever sins has neither seen Him nor known Him. Little children, let no one deceive you. He who practices righteousness is righteous, just as He is righteous. He*

who sins is of the devil, for the devil has sinned from the beginning. For this purpose the Son of God was manifested, that He might destroy the works of the devil. Whoever has been born of God does not sin, for His seed remains in him; and he cannot sin, because he has been born of God. In this the children of God and the children of the devil are manifest: Whoever does not practice righteousness is not of God, nor is he who does not love his brother (1 John 3:4-10).

By this we know that we love the children of God, when we love God and keep His commandments. For this is the love of God, that we keep His commandments. And His commandments are not burdensome (1 John 5:2-3).

Though the hyper grace teachers try to reason their way around these and other scriptures the message is quite clear. Professing to know God but not keeping His commandments is not the religion of the Bible. The apostles John and James were not alone among Bible writers in confronting this false teaching that has now also swept through major segments of the Nigerian Church. Paul warned the Corinthians to not even associate with so-called brothers or sisters if they were in any way immoral, or covetous, or drunkards, etc. (see 1 Corinthians 5:1-12), showing us clearly that careful obedience to God and to His scriptural commandments are fundamental to Christian life and indeed to our eternal salvation. Clearly hyper grace is not just hyper; it is false.

One of the most dangerous teachings of the hyper grace movement is that they dismiss major portions of the Bible as irrelevant to our own day. They throw out the relevancy of Old Testament teachings (including the Ten Commandments), as well as any teachings of Jesus before His resurrection. They tell us that none of this applies to believers today. However, in

Mark 13:31, Jesus said, *"Heaven and earth will pass away, but my words will never pass away."* Before Jesus ascended into heaven, He promised that the Father would send the Holy Spirit who *"will teach you all things and will remind you of everything I have said to you"* (John 14:26). If Jesus' words are no longer applicable to believers, why would we need to be reminded of them?

In the Great Commission, given after the resurrection, Jesus instructed His disciples to teach their followers to obey all things He had commanded them. Since this instruction was given after the resurrection, it should be binding on those who hold this view, if they are to be consistent. Yet, it required that the new believers be taught to observe all things that Jesus had earlier taught.

Hyper grace teaching is an example of mixing truth with error. We have already noted that this is *always* true of Satan's theological seduction. Such teaching does have an understandable appeal to people who have been badgered by over-zealous legalism that has left them with a perpetual feeling of false guilt. Many are starved for a correct understanding of Bible truth about grace. Therefore, the hyper grace message of total freedom in Christ is very appealing. An emphasis on the beauty and power of God's grace is good. However, in the process the hyper grace people neglect what Paul calls the *"whole counsel of God"* (Acts 20:27). For example, though it is true that Christians have been forgiven by God that does not mean that as believers we never have to confess our sins.

It is hard to deny the fact that 1 John 1:9 gives clear instruction to believers about confessing sin. It begins with the word *if*: *"If we confess our sins, He is faithful and just to forgive us our sins and to cleanse us from all unrighteousness."* We must bear in mind, of course, that John goes ahead immediately at the beginning of the next chapter to say that he does not accept sinning as normative for healthy Christian living (*"My little children, these things I write to you, so that you may not sin"* [1 John 2:1]). Sinning i.e., walking in willful disobedience to God is normative for the unsaved, but never for believers.

Nevertheless, 1 John 1:9 says that when we do sin we must confess it to God, and then know that he is faithful and just to forgive us. This is a cause/effect statement implying that we cannot experience God's forgiveness without first confessing our sins. As blood-bought children of God, we do not continue to confess our sin in order to be saved from hell. Rather, we confess and repent in order to reestablish an intimate relationship with our Father. We are "positionally righteous" but "practically sinful," yet without confession we run the risk of falling into a backslidden and potentially fatal position.

To counter this argument, hyper grace preachers deny that John's letters were written to believers. However, 1 John 2:1says clearly, *"My little children, these things I write to you, so that you may not sin. And if anyone sins, we have an Advocate with the Father, Jesus Christ the righteous."* John is clearly writing to believers whom he personally knew, and affectionately refers to them as his children. He indicates that his believing hearers may indeed sin, and that, when they do, they need to confess it.

Hypergrace preachers also claim the Holy Spirit will never convict Christians of their sin. Mature Christians should recognize this quickly, judging not only from scripture but also from their personal experience. Without exception, every disciple of Christ has felt the persistent and patient conviction of the Holy Spirit when he or she has sinned. This is one of the reasons Jesus calls the Holy Spirit *"the Spirit of Truth"* (John 15:26). Truth, by definition, will not tolerate anything false. Therefore, when the Spirit of Truth abides in a believing heart (1 Corinthians 6:19), he brings conviction about anything that is *not* truth.

There is no doubt that much of hyper grace teaching is valid. As we have noted, the focus on freedom in Christ, through grace, is commendable. We are indeed saved by grace, and not by works (Ephesians 2:89). God's grace is marvelous, great, and free (1 Timothy 1:14). However, hyper grace teaching is taught in an exaggerated form and all too frequently out of harmony with the rest of scripture. When any doctrine is emphasized to the exclusion of other key doctrines, we fall into error because we fail to *"correctly handle"* God's word (2 Timothy 2:15).

John noted that Jesus, the Word made flesh, was full of both "grace and truth" (John 1:14). Those two attributes must always be kept in delicate balance. Leaning too far to either side will produce error. That is why it is essential for the Church to insist on excellent biblical and theological training for its leadership. They must be men and women who have the capacity to always compare any new teaching with the "whole counsel of God" and learn to disregard anything that deviates in any way from the center of God's revealed truth (1 John 4:1).

There is a great need for the Nigerian Church to be more faithfully nurtured in sound doctrinal and biblical preaching. Much too often our pulpits resound with shallow preaching that satisfies itching ears of people longing for worldly success but who are not willing to deny themselves, take up their crosses and follow Jesus. The often-shallow euphoria that characterizes too many of our assemblies is a sign of the times. The problem is that our cheap and often tawdry triumphalism will not get us to heaven or even give us lasting joy and peace on earth.

Furthermore, many churches and preachers these days refuse to take a stand against sin and rarely if ever mention the need for repentance or topics like hell and judgment. If there is anything we can learn from examining the function of Bible prophets it is that they never hesitated to pronounce the judgments of God against the sins of His people. Such people are today in short supply within the Nigerian Church. Many of our churches allow people to minister in music, as small group leaders and even as pulpit ministers with no personal accountability while looking the other way as they live sexually immoral lives and regularly engage in drunkenness!

Solomon reminded us long ago, *"there is nothing new under the sun"*(Ecclesiastes 1:9).For centuries the body of Christ has wrestled with antinomianism. The idea that the moral laws of God no longer apply to us and that free grace allows us to live any way we like has been a perennial problem down through the ages. Yet this is not the message of the Bible. Paul asks rhetorically in Romans 6:1, *"Shall we continue in sin that grace may abound?"* His thunderous response is: *"God forbid! How shall we that are dead to sin live any longer in it?"*

THE TELLTALE SIGNS

In concluding this chapter we wish to highlight what we believe are principal telltale signs of the erroneous hyper grace teaching. Without impugning either the character or the motives of those who have embraced this teaching we note five things that should raise red flags in our minds when we hear this teaching. There are other signs that could be mentioned, of course. And not all of these signs are equally manifested among hyper grace teachers, but each should give us pause for consideration, and a reminder to contend for the faith once and for all delivered to the saints.

Major portions of the Bible are neglected or discounted. Marcion, who was born in 85 AD while the last of the original apostles, John, was still living, taught that the God of the Old Testament was different from the Father of Jesus Christ. He therefore rejected the Old Testament and accepted only parts of the New Testament. His teachings were denounced by the Church Fathers. It would not be unfair to label hyper grace teaching as repetitive of this ancient heresy. In varying degrees they regard the authority of the Old Testament as irrelevant to our modern lives.

However, Paul says emphatically in 2 Timothy 3:16 that *"All scripture is given by inspiration of God, and is profitable for doctrine, for reproof, for correction, for instruction in righteousness."* The neglecting of the Old Testament and rejection of the pre-resurrection teachings of Jesus Christ as irrelevant or even secondary to today's believers is a serious error. It is contrary to historic understanding of the Church.

> **REALITY CHECK:** Any theology that discards or discounts parts of the Holy Bible as irrelevant or unimportant is not sound. All scripture is God-breathed, and all scripture is profitable.

Sometimes hyper grace preachers do preach from Old Testament texts, but they treat the Old Testament only as types and shadows that are useful for sermon illustrations but that do not give guidelines for our lives. However, a proper understanding is that the Old Testament and the New Testament speak with a single voice and a common message.

They do not contradict each other, and together provide the necessary foundation for our lives.

The topic of sin is seldom mentioned. If hyper grace preachers mention sin it is almost never in the sense of taking a stand against the popular sins of the day. Therefore, their teaching on repentance is shallow and omits the Bible focus on repentance as godly sorrow for sin. They can go on and on about the sin of legalism or Phariseeism, of course, but when it comes to the concept of rebellion against God they tend to be silent. And of course they have little to say in rebuke of sin among believers.

Contrary to the hyper grace teachers, one point of commendation for many of the Word of Faith teachers is a strong focus on the importance of avoiding sin. David Oyedepo and E. A. Adeboye, both of whom have become strong advocates for the theology of Kenneth Hagin and its faulty concepts of faith and prosperity, nevertheless are to be highly commended as strong proponents of the need for holy living and the avoidance of sin. Johnson Odesola's testimony about Adeboye is that *"holiness remains the hallmark of his lifestyle and messages."*[120]

REALITY CHECK: One of the surest ways to discover the truth of any theological system is to examine their doctrine of sin. Paul said that the first thing grace teaches us is to *"deny ungodliness and worldly lusts"* (Titus 2:12). Churches without a strong message against sin are not preaching the whole counsel of God.

One of the hallmarks of Bible prophets and preachers, as well as of the great revivalists in the history of the Church, is that

---

[120]Johnson Funso Odesola, *Apostle of Holiness: An Expose on E. A. Adeboye's Holiness Concepts,* 2012, Dynamic ERA Global Services Ltd, Lagos, Nigeria, p. 33.

they always preached pointedly and strongly against the sins of their day. They were sensitive to the cultural issues around them and spoke out against current expressions of rebellion against God. By contrast, many of the hyper grace teachers tend to avoid topics such as abortion, homosexuality, pornography, masturbation and pre-marital sex, perhaps out of fear of offending their hearers.

One of the reasons this is true is that these preachers like to tell us that God is always in a good mood, and therefore He is always pleased with us. They portray Him as a doting father who is never perturbed by the misbehavior of His children. However, it is easy to overlook the fact that though God is "good all the time" he never fails to hold His children accountable and He never ceases to be angry against sin. Apparently the hyper grace God has received anger-management therapy and is therefore always in a good mood. This is not the teaching of the Bible.

There is a tendency to preach only positive and motivational sermons. Hyper grace theology is an interesting combination of Marcionism, Word of Faith, and once-saved-always-saved Calvinism. People such as Joseph Prince and Joel Osteen put it all in a big theological pot, stir it up, and dish it out. But the practical result in hyper grace preaching is that it is usually highly positive and motivational. God loves you, He is happy with you, He has forgiven you, and He wants to give you all kinds of prosperity. All of those things are part of the message of the Bible, but when we do not preach and teach the whole counsel of God it is like feeding our children with a strict diet of sugar and honey. It will not end well.

Here's the way Paul put it, talking to the elders of the Ephesians church: *"Therefore I testify to you this day that I am innocent of the blood of all men. For I have not shunned to declare to you the whole counsel of God"* (Acts 20:26-27). The "whole counsel" of God means that we must give our people more than just feel-good messages. We must do this so that we are innocent from the blood of all men (Acts 20:26-27).

People of questionable morality or ethics are often allowed to teach or hold key posts. It is a sad commentary on contemporary evangelical churches virtually around the world that sexual immorality, drunkenness and other forms of worldly pleasure seeking are on the rise. In too many hyper grace churches the leaders see little or nor problem with things like drunkenness, profanity, vulgarity, bribery, divorce, etc. Because there is a strong emphasis on grace and no teaching against sin or on repentance, judgment or hell there is often an atmosphere of loose living. This is not the religion of the Bible.

What many may not realize is that if the moral law of the scriptures is not faithfully preached our people will inevitably go astray. This includes such basics as the Ten Commandments, which are as fundamentally applicable to God's people today as they were on the day God gave them to Moses. Where such teaching is absent people descend into foolish living and blind leaders end up leading blind people. Proverbs 28:18 says it well: *"Where there is no revelation, the people cast off restraint; but happy is he who keeps the law."* In other words, where there is no clear teaching of God's law the people tend to live unbridled and godless lives.

Charismatic scholar and apologist Michael L. Brown has written passionately about the challenge of this new teaching. He notes *"It is increasingly common to hear about worship leaders getting drunk after church services and dropping f-bombs while they boast about their 'liberty' in the Lord."*

There is no clear teaching on the doctrine of holiness or sanctification. As a part of their acceptance of Reformed teaching, hyper grace teachers reject any ideas of ongoing sanctification in the life of believers in favor of the concept of positional sanctification. Positional sanctification is the teaching that believers are entirely covered by the righteousness of Christ when they are born again and therefore when God looks at them he sees not their own character but only the character of Christ. They are pure and holy because of the purity and holiness of Christ. They are as holy as they will ever be.

They therefore totally reject the idea that believers should pursue a life of practical holiness, because that would imply that God does not already see them as holy. Further, there is nothing they can ever do that would cause them to miss heaven no matter how egregious it may be. As Joseph Prince says, *"Because you did nothing to deserve His presence in your life, there is nothing you can do that will cause His presence to leave you."* [121]

However, as we are saying repeatedly in this book, the sanctification of believers is one of the most foundational teachings of the New Testament. The sanctification of believers is both instantaneous (1 Thessalonians 5:23) and gradual (Hebrews 10:14; Philippians 3:12-15). In other words, there are one or more points of momentary cleansing in the hearts of seeking believers, when the Holy Spirit convicts them of issues of impurity in their hearts and gives them a deeper cleansing.

---

[121] Joseph Prince, Facebook, June 19, 2013, https://www.facebook.com/josephprince/posts/532289340152253, accessed 18 January 2017.

Sanctification is also an ongoing process in the life of believers in which they are transformed more and more into the image and character of Christ. We are not talking about some kind of legal change here, but true moral transformation, in which issues of our sinful nature are dealt with sometimes very painfully and we are morally transformed. We must never forget that both justification and sanctification involve much more than a mere change in legal status before God. The result is a changed lifestyle of good works, as we are reminded of repeatedly in the scriptures (James 2:14-26).

Unfortunately, hyper grace teachers tend to denounce the scriptural call for pursuing ethical standards of holy living as legalism, or attempting to earn salvation through our meritorious works. However, it is not legalism for Christians to keep the commandments, and Jesus not only said that he did not come to destroy the law (Matthew 5:17) but he said, *"If you love Me, keep My commandments"* (John 14:15).

> **REALITY CHECK:** The bedrock of divine revelation is the call of God for a holy people — *"but as He who called you is holy, you also be holy in all your conduct, because it is written, "Be holy, for I am holy"* (1 Peter 1:15-16). Diminishing the scriptural demand for sanctification and for holy living is a major hallmark of modern apostasy.

Vic Reasoner has warned against the excesses included in this teaching of what he calls counterfeit grace, combining the errors of the distorted prosperity gospel with a modern form of antinomianism.[122] He points out numerous errors within the movement, and notes that all of the errors are repetitions of false teachings that have cropped up in the Church time and

---

[122]Vic Reasoner, "Counterfeit Grace," *The Arminian Magazine*, Issue 1-2, Spring & Fall, 2015, Vol. 33, pp. 4-5.

again over the centuries. This is one more reminder that sound theological and biblical training, plus a thorough grasp of the history of the Church, is essential for safeguarding us against these and others areas. May God help us.

Paul reminds us in Titus 2:11-14 that true grace teaches us to say "No" to ungodliness and worldly passions and to live self-controlled, upright and godly lives in this present age. Grace is the unmerited gift of God, and the gift He gives us instructs us. To be able to say "No" to sin, one has to have seen his relationship with God. Sin often arises when we feel a need and then conclude that the only way to meet that need is outside what God has revealed as acceptable. However, when we come to the realization that God is now our Father in the best sense of that word, we know that He will meet all our genuine needs. This ability is absolutely unlimited.

Therefore, we can trust that He will provide whatever it is that we feel as a need, if it is genuine. When we trust Him in that way, we shall have no need to go outside what God permits in order to meet our need. Thus, by reminding us of our child/Father relationship with God and its full implications, grace teaches us to reject sin and worldly passions and to live self-controlled and upright lives here and now.

If we do that we will not find ourselves comfortable listening to the preachers of hyper grace, but we will surely find ourselves properly dressed and ready when our God and Savior Jesus Christ returns.

RECOVERING TRUNCATED REVIVALS AND HOLY MANDATES

This book must end on a positive note. A primary reason is that the Bible itself ends on a positive note. The Kingdom of God will always triumph in the end. It was prophesied right from the Old Testament *("of the increase of His government and peace there shall be no end,"* [Isaiah 9:7]), and is proclaimed in the final words of the New Testament *("They shall reign forever and ever,"* [Revelation 22:5]). This is why the reviving of the Church and return to biblical orthodoxy is dear to the heart of God. It is true that today Satan is a formidable foe, but all power in heaven and earth is given to Jesus. No matter how fierce the opposition, truth will win decisively in the end. No matter how fierce and prolonged the battle, we have every right to claim that same victory in the case of the battle for the soul of the Nigerian Church.

Though it is true that the Nigerian Church has been tragically lured away from solid scriptural and theological foundations over the past forty years we believe there is great hope for reformation and revival. It will not happen automatically or even by some kind of sovereign divine declaration. It will also require us to do our part. We cannot sit down and fold our hands on the assumption that it will happen automatically.

That is the reason we repeat once again our deep conviction that the biblical revival for which we have long prayed and believed may not come unless and until we own up to the errors we have embraced. Full victory will not likely come until we identify and discard erroneous teachings and habits that have held back the revival blessings of God Almighty.

It is clear to us that as never before the Nigerian Church is in need of true prophets who proclaim the word of God without fear. We need men and women who, like Martin Luther, will prophetically face the wrath of reigning popes big and small all over the land. As we write this we are now in the year celebrating the 500th anniversary of Luther's 1517 bold moves toward reformation. And today, once again, the Nigerian Church faces a pervasive need for reformation - church leadership, church structures, church theology, church education, church worship, church prayer, etc.

HOW DO WE RECOVER BIBLE FOUNDATIONS?

The primary key is the recovery of Bible foundations threatened and weakened over the past generation. We must return to the Bible itself reading and studying it afresh and letting it speak for itself without imported interpretations from dubious outside sources. Every year there are more Nigerian pastors and teachers who are competent in the biblical languages, who have a grasp of the history of Christian orthodoxy, and who are led by the Spirit of God. We are more than capable to do the self-theologizing that is important for all mature churches around the world.

For many decades God used the ministry of the Scripture Union to inculcate a strong focus on the Bible all across this country. It left a mark on Nigeria hardly paralleled anywhere else in the world. The Scripture Union was established in 1867 in Britain and brought to Nigeria in 1884. It rose to its most effective height here in the 1950s and beyond, with its ubiquitous Bible reading cards, all over the nation.[123] We must get back to that basic fascination with the written word of God and once again renew our thirst to let the Bible speak to us in its own terms. We must throw away any ideas that some parts of the Bible are not for us, but for a different age, accepting the fact that *all* scripture is God-breathed.

There is no greater antidote to false teaching than a strong focus on the truth of God's word. The scriptures give us guidelines on how to confront false teaching, in part because several of the Bible writers wrote to directly confront errors prevalent in their own day. We can still learn from them, because many of the errors we face today are a replay of what they experienced. Paul confronted false teachings in the Mediterranean world of his day, and was especially vigilant against the threat of Jewish legalism. In the book of Romans he also confronted the antinomianism of his day.

Peter's second epistle is a good example of his own efforts to speak out against false teachings. His first letter dealt largely with problems outside the Church, but in his second letter he warned about false teachers who were destroying the flock through their enticing false teaching. It is particularly noteworthy that Peter began his second letter by imploring his hearers to take heed about their own personal lives, and that they ensure that they were pursuing moral excellence, knowledge, self-control, godliness, etc.

---

[123] D. Maduako (et al), *Flame of Fire: The Story of the Scripture Union (Nigeria)* (Ibadan: Scripture Union Press, 2005); John Charles Pollock, *The Good Seed: The Story of the Children's Special Service Mission and the Scripture Union* (London: Hodder and Stoughton, 1959); Gary S. Maxey, *Capturing a Lost Vision: Can Nigeria's Greatest Revival Live Again?* (Lagos: WATS Publications, 2016), pp. 53-57.

Peter understood clearly the goal of holiness of heart and life, as he had plainly told his hearers in his first letter repeating God's command for them to be holy (1 Peter 1:15-16).If we can understand in our own day that we, too, must pursue holiness of heart and life as preparation to confront error that will go a long way to our full victory.

In his second letter Peter reminded them that their goal should be literally to be *"partakers of the divine nature"* (i.e., holiness), having *"escaped the corruption that is in the world through lust"* (i.e., fleshly desires, 2 Peter 1:4). Following that God-ordained path obviously put them in total contrast to the false teachers who were sensual, arrogant, and greedy (2 Peter 2:3. 12-22). Such people, Peter noted, have no time to think about future judgment but rather prefer to focus on the here and now.

Within the scriptures, that focus on the world to come was one of the motivating factors for present holiness of heart and life. As we have already pointed out, one of the enemy's strategies in the seduction of the Nigerian Church is to lure us away from focusing on the world to come as the basis of our Christianity. But this is really a core value. As Paul said, *"if in this life only we have hope in Christ, then we are of all men most to be pitied"* (1 Corinthians 15:19).

We have already noted that the Civil War Revival in Nigeria was propelled on the winds of the expectation of the soon return of Christ and the dawn of the eternal life that it promised. Our focus on heaven needs to be unapologetically restored. The end of life in this world is the most certain thing for anyone alive. If we do not focus on preparing for what lies beyond it, then we are most unwise indeed. Listen to Peter once again:

> *Therefore, since all these things will be dissolved, what manner of persons ought you to be in holy conduct and godliness, looking for and hastening the coming of the day of God. . . . be diligent to be found by Him in peace, without spot and blameless. . . . because lest you also fall from your own steadfastness, being led away with the error of the wicked* (2 Peter 3:11-12, 14, 17).

The parallels with our own day here in Nigeria are striking. It serves to underscore our point that getting a stronger grasp on the Bible is the surest foundation for the contemporary Nigerian Church to confront error and to pave the way toward genuine revival. We should not be surprised that some of the contemporary doctrines holding sway in Nigeria encourage people to discount major portions of the Bible, as we have seen with the hyper grace teachers. That is exceedingly dangerous and should be soundly rejected.

In other cases, we are told that God has called certain church groups to focus almost exclusive attention on single scriptural themes, such as healing, or deliverance, or material prosperity. The result is that millions of Nigerian believers are left with a precariously unbalanced theological and biblical diet. Under those circumstances members tend to be lop-sided and unavoidably anemic spiritually. They are also thereby vulnerable to distortions that rob us all of the revival we so desperately lack.

The need is to return to the whole counsel of God, just as Paul exhorted in his final address to the elders of Ephesus:

> *For I have not shunned to declare to you the whole counsel of God. Therefore take heed to yourselves and to all the flock, . . . For I know this, that after my departure savage wolves will come in among you, not sparing the flock. . . . speaking perverse*

things, to draw away the disciples after themselves. (Acts 20:27-30).

REJECTION OF FALSE TEACHING

Our need is not only to return to the solid meat of the Bible but also to specifically and strategically confront and reject false teachings that have overtaken the Nigerian Church. We must not be timid or unduly diplomatic about this. This involves knowledgeable and bold refutation of biblical and theological errors wherever they surface, including the false doctrines we have pointed out in previous chapters.

The unbalanced prosperity message must be unmasked for what it is a distortion of biblical teaching that caters to ungodly human greed and self-centeredness. Teachers of this false gospel have at times made the exaggerated or distorted claim that their opponents teach poverty as a virtue or that it is sinful to have money or material goods. But that is not true. The Bible neither condemns money per se nor does it say that wealth is morally wrong. But it does most strongly warn against the love of money and the desire to be rich for its own sake.

We must be bold to reject this common error among us, no matter who is "pulling crowd" with it. It is painful that we now have a situation in Nigeria where, in direct opposition to the teachings of scripture, contemporary Nigerian Church leaders often say things such as, *"Many are ignorant of the fact that God has already made provision for His children to be wealthy here on earth. When I say wealth, I mean very, very rich. . . . Break loose! It is not a sin to desire to be wealthy."* [124] That type of teaching must be soundly rejected.

---

[124] Isaac Phiri and Joe Maxwell, "Gospel Riches: Africa's rapid embrace of prosperity Pentecostalism provokes concern and hope," *Christianity Today*, July 2007, Vol. 57, No. 7, p. 22.

We must turn away from the enticement of money and from teaching that focuses on wealth as a primary goal. If we understand biblical stewardship properly we will know that the only reason God gives some of us more than we need materially is so we can help others and expand the kingdom of God, and not so we can consume it on ourselves in progressively more lavish lifestyles or so we can pile it up in larger and larger quantities.

We must therefore raise collective voices against Church leaders who do not set a godly example through selfless and humble lifestyles. Laying up treasures on earth is directly contradictory to the teaching of Jesus, no matter who is doing it. We must return to the former standards where Church leaders who accumulate large personal wealth seek to give away most of what they have to help those in need and to serve as an example of personal frugality and generosity to those around them.

The intrusion of African Traditional Religion into the Church must be likewise rejected. Instances of blatant appeal to overt occultism within the Church, including pacts with demonic spirits, blood sacrifices, use of charms, etc., must be identified clearly as the property and territory of Satan, and not of God. The seeking of any kind of power through the use of material objects has no place in a Bible-centered Church, whether in the form of blessed water, anointing oil, handkerchiefs, or whatever else. Pronouncing of curses on other people must be recognized as the non-Christian and non-biblical practice that it truly is, no matter how widely it may be practiced. We must learn how to avoid anything that takes our focus away from Jesus Christ and his love and power and sovereignty and puts it on human beings or material objects of any kind.

The idea that we through any kind of godlike fiat can manipulate power must be avoided. Prayer must not focus on human beings pronouncing decrees or commanding spirits or speaking things into existence. Rather, our focus must be about humble reliance on the power of Almighty God, based on our relationship with Jesus Christ through divine grace. We must learn to use more second-person pronouns rather than first-person pronouns in our prayers. Our prayers need less of "I command," or "I decree," or "I send fire," and more of "Your kingdom come," "Your will be done," and "give us this day."

We need another E. M. Bounds to bless the Nigerian Church. That great master teacher about prayer of over 100 years ago is needed now more than ever. Any pastor who determinedly soaks himself in the works of E. M. Bounds on prayer will come out of the prayer closet as a new person. Consider a small sampling:

> *Our praying suffers as much as our religion from bad living. Preachers were charged in primitive times to preach by their lives or preach not at all. So Christians everywhere ought to be charged to pray by their lives or pray not at all. . . . Praying which does not result in pure conduct is a delusion. We have missed the whole office and virtue of praying if it does not rectify conduct. It is in the very nature of things that we must quit praying or quit bad conduct. Cold, dead praying may exist with bad conduct, but cold, dead praying is no praying in God's esteem. Our praying advances in power as it rectifies the life. . . . One of the first necessities, if we are to grasp the infinite possibilities of prayer, is to get rid of prayerless praying.* [125]

---

[125] E. M. Bounds, *The Complete Collection of E. M. Bounds on Prayer* (Wilder Publications, 2009), *passim*.

We must learn how to identify the false teaching that the grace of God can lead to a life of carelessness over the issue of sin and obedience. It is true that the entrance into the heavenly kingdom is by grace, but we must never forget that our walk with God is by obedience day after day. Grace is God's part; obedience is our part. The true work of grace is to teach us how to obey rather than to absolve us of the need to obey. Or, to put it another way, we are not saved *by* works, but we are saved *unto* works.

True faith in God results in "new creatures" (2 Corinthians 5:17) who then go on to live godly and obedient lives. God does not expect us to live in sinless perfection. That is the reason why he made provision for repentance and cleansing for us when we do sin. However, he does expect us to live godly and holy lives (or, as Paul would say it, to be "saints," or holy ones).

The scriptures are quite clear: *"he that practices righteousness is righteous, just as He is righteous"* (1 John 3:7). And at the risk of repetition we say that we must also stand firm on our conviction that *"**All** Scripture is given by inspiration of God, and is profitable for doctrine, for reproof, for correction, for instruction in righteousness"* (2 Timothy 3:16). We are not free to determine that certain portions of the scripture are not as authoritative as others or are not for our own edification.

Our boldness in confronting these and other biblical and theological errors in the Nigerian Church is essential for our survival and for the role God has laid out for us in global Christian leadership. We are strongly convinced that the African Church will set the agenda for global Christianity in this century with the Nigerian Church at the forefront and it can only do so responsibly by confronting any errors that hinder its faithfulness in that assignment.

EMBRACING SOUND BIBLE INTERPRETATION

Paul's exhortation in 2 Timothy 2:15 is to *"Be diligent to present yourself approved to God, a worker who does not need to be ashamed, rightly dividing the word of truth."* The concept behind "be diligent" is to strive with all our energies. (The KJV *"study* to show yourself approved" reflects a change in an English language word over the past 400 years and has no reference to academic studying, as we tend to hear it today.) Eugene Peterson, in his own paraphrase, *The Message*, renders it *"concentrate on doing your best for God."* In short, it takes concerted effort for any of us to rightly understand the truth of the scriptures.

Thankfully, down through the centuries competent scholars within the Church have established universally recognized principles of sound Bible interpretation that we must not ignore. Yet today the Nigerian Church is awash with popular misinterpretations of scripture that have aided and abetted the spread of false theologies and have lent credibility to the errors about which we have been writing.

This is why we believe it is high time for concerted efforts to ensure that we return to sound hermeneutics and sound Bible teaching. The establishment of one or more high-level interchurch commissions to address these issues would be a welcome development, and perhaps even a necessary expedient to usher in reformation and revival.

It is common for those who have not been properly trained in the field of Bible interpretation to use the scriptures to proof-text ideas and theologies they want to support. It is regrettable that leaders within both the Word of Faith and hyper grace movements do this sort of thing with wearying frequency. At times they give the appearance of expertise in Bible teaching, yet they frequently quote scriptures out of context and make false claims about the original Bible languages.

Often they fail to distinguish between *eisegesis* and *exegesis*. *Eisegesis* (literally, "leading in") is the illegitimate practice of reading our own meaning or interpretation into scripture and should always be avoided as much as possible. On the other hand, *exegesis* ("leading out") is the legitimate and necessary practice of discovering the meaning that is there in the God-breathed scripture, and bringing it out clearly.

Good exegesis is not easy. It requires long hours and even long weeks and months to properly master. It must be guided by the Holy Spirit but also without bypassing the sweat and toil that is required to become proficient in any worthwhile skill. Pastors and church leaders who closet themselves with the Lord and who tarry for endowment with wisdom and power and understanding are to be commended. But we must also remember that there is no substitute for the hard work of thoroughly learning the time-tested rules of Bible interpretation. We must therefore move beyond the syndrome of self-appointed leaders without clear understanding of Bible exegesis locking themselves into isolated rooms for days listening to or reading about new "revelations" from here or there and then emerging with claims that they are now trained by the Holy Spirit. As Ali notes, *"Ironically, some who desire to train others now, never submitted their lives under their elders to be taught, discipled or trained. What a contradiction! They told us the Holy Spirit trained them."*[126]

---

[126] Ali, *Op cit.*, pp. 31-32.

Thankfully our misinterpretations of the Bible are not as bad as some we have heard of, such as the man who swore that the wearing of neckties is forbidden in scripture. He based it on his reading of Malachi's command to *"Bring all of the **ties** into the storehouse."* We also heard about an unrepentant kleptomaniac who changed the punctuation of Ephesians 4:28 a bit to read, *"Let him who stole, steal; no more working with his hands."*

Of course those examples are only pulpit humor. But there are more serious misreadings of the Bible that have in several cases become almost sacred truth here in Nigeria as a result of constant repetition over a period of years. The King James Version translation of Isaiah 45:11 is a case in point. It says, *"Thus saith the LORD, the Holy One of Israel, and his Maker, Ask me of things to come concerning my sons, and concerning the work of my hands command ye me."* A superficial reading of that verse out of context, and erroneously assuming that the verb "command" must be in the imperative mood appears to support the idea that we have the capacity as humans to command God to do whatever we want Him to do. It is on the basis of that quite faulty interpretation that multitudes have presumed that commanding and decreeing is a legitimate practice in prayer, which it most definitely is not.

The truth is that Isaiah 45 says the exact opposite of what is alleged. The New King James Version makes it clear that "command" is not an imperative verb, but rather declarative: *"concerning the work of My hands, you command Me."* When we look at a sampling of other translations it becomes even clearer. The New English Translation (NET) says, *"How dare you tell me what to do with the work of my own hands!"* And the Good News Translation (GNT) says, *"You have no right to question me about my children or to tell me what I ought to do!"* Obviously, God is warning us not to try to command Him, since He alone is God.

The context of Isaiah 45:11 makes this common misinterpretation even more plain. Reading Isaiah 45:9-11 in the Good News Translation reads:

> *⁹ Does a clay pot dare argue with its maker,*
> *a pot that is like all the others?*
> *Does the clay ask the potter what he is doing?*
> *Does the pot complain that its maker has no skill?*
>
> *¹⁰ Do we dare say to our parents,*
> *"Why did you make me like this?"*
>
> *¹¹ The Lord, the holy God of Israel,*
> *the one who shapes the future, says:*
> *"You have no right to question me about my children*
> *Or to tell me what I ought to do!*

2 John 3 is an example of another scripture that is frequently interpreted out of context, especially by those in the Word of Faith movement. It may well be the most widely quoted verse among the health and wealth advocates: *"Beloved, I wish above all things that thou mayest prosper and be in health, even as thy soul prospereth"* (KJV). Reading this verse out of context has landed many in trouble. The context of this verse is a common First-Century greeting in which the writer wishes good physical health to the readers. It has absolutely nothing to do with the issue of material prosperity, and suggesting otherwise would be a classic example of the eisegesis we mentioned earlier. The GNT translation gets closer to the simple meaning here: *"My dear friend, I pray that everything may go well with you and that you may be in good health as I know you are well in spirit."* To extrapolate from this verse the idea that God desires for all of His children to be financially or materially blessed is a serious abuse of scripture.

This is not the place to give a comprehensive list of faulty hermeneutics going on in our churches, though a concise compendium of such abuses would be helpful. Our conviction is that this is an issue that we must not avoid if we expect to see genuine reformation and revival in the Nigerian Church.

Renewed Call for Repentance and Seeking the Face of God

Genuine revival always begins with a sense of acute need. This is confirmed both within scripture and within the pages of Church history. The undeniable truth is that the Holy Spirit does not revive people who believe they are doing great and who have no need of serious spiritual improvement. That is why we have continued to speak out against the attitude of cheap triumphalism that characterizes many of our meetings.

Those among us who are sensitive to the Holy Spirit, however, know that there is a great need for revival in the Nigerian Church. We know that the Holy Spirit is grieved with our shallowness and our pride. They know that in many ways things are worse now than they were several years back. We are in an age of too much backsliddenness and shallow Christian living. And we have succumbed to worldliness and greed in a way never before seen.

That is why one of the great needs of our day is a fresh spirit of repentance and of seeking the face of Almighty God. The message of 2 Chronicles 7:14 is as relevant today as ever: *"If My people who are called by My name will humble themselves, and pray and seek My face, and turn from their wicked ways, then I will hear from heaven, and will forgive their sin and heal their land."*

Those of us who know the history of how the fire of the Civil War Revival was eventually lost can pray knowledgeably about God's forgiveness over our backsliding as a Nigerian Church. We can pray that kind of prayer as a form of identificational repentance. What we mean by that is to follow the example of Old Testament prophets who prayed to God in agonies over the sins of their nation, but who did so not in the third person, but in the first person. It was not *"Lord, they have sinned,"* but *"Lord, I and my people have sinned."*

The prayer of Daniel is very instructive here (Daniel 9:15):

> *And I prayed to the Lord my God, and made confession, and said, "O Lord, great and awesome God, who keeps His covenant and mercy with those who love Him, and with those who keep His commandments, we have sinned and committed iniquity, we have done wickedly and rebelled, even by departing from Your precepts and Your judgments.*

One member of the Concerned Ministers Forum, Dennis Nweke, notes that with the loss of this kind of repentant attitude that was universally shared during the Civil War Revival, the eventual result was schism and discord and self-centered drives toward independency. The focus shifted away from genuine repentance and revival toward more focus on the building of personal ecclesiastical empires.

> *All those who witnessed the move of the Holy Ghost in Nigeria in the early seventies (precisely 1969-1973) will attest to the joy, unfettered fellowship, great conversions, signs and wonders that characterized that move. Unfortunately, we lost that move partly due to the selfishness and greed of some of the key players, who, not satisfied to have the fellowship as the Holy Ghost was directing, cut out chunks of the body to build personal empires and gathered to themselves a following. This unfortunate*

development fragmented the body of believers, bringing with it schisms and discord, bickerings and rancor. Gradually but steadily, with time, the fire died.[127]

Our fear is that even today instead of acknowledging our backslidings and lukewarmness many of us are too busy imploring God for greater material and social prosperity. And because of the itching ears of the people there are fewer preachers these days willing to preach true repentance. We have noted the hyper grace tendency to reduce repentance to mere mental consent, while bypassing focus on godly sorrow as a scriptural measurement for it. Speaking of the danger of conversion without true repentance, The Concerned Ministers Forum notes:

What makes matters worse is the tendency of these preachers to ignore true repentance. In this false doctrine, people are made Christian because they changed their minds to come to church. As newcomers to church, they are prayed for and received as Christians. . . . [But] until a man turns away from sin, and turns to God wholeheartedly, he cannot be a Christian. These days, preachers who want to attract and retain the crowd by all means, deliberately neglect to emphasize the true repentance necessary for real conversion.[128]

ESTABLISHING SOUND BIBLICAL AND THEOLOGICAL TRAINING

Henry Venn, the indefatigable British leader of the Church Missionary Society from 1842 to 1873, is credited with establishing the familiar three-fold criterion for measuring the viability of Christian movements emerging among non-

---

[127] Dennis Nweke, *Contending*, p. 72.
[128] Onofurho, *Contending*, p. 56.

Christian populations around the world. Such movements, according to Venn, should be self-governing, self-financing and self-propagating. However, this time-honored standard omitted one other measure of maturity, and that is the need for self-theologizing.

What this means is that strong and mature Christian churches must not only be capable of governing themselves, providing their own financial survival, and capable of reproducing themselves in perpetuity. They must also be able to sustain and perpetuate faithful Bible exegesis and biblical and systematic theology within their own environment. Without paying the price to develop those capabilities coupled with the powerful anointing of the Holy Spirit the Church will be in constant risk of deception and error and vulnerable to outside theological pressures.

We must be blunt to say that the Nigerian Church has paid a heavy price for its failure to take the theological task more seriously. The failure to demand and provide for the cultivation and training of indigenous Bible scholars and theologians and to place them in positions of respect and influence has come at a sad cost. The failure to provide for or demand basic theological training for wide swaths of Nigerian church leaders has left the Church repeatedly vulnerable to imported heretical teaching.

The decentralization of church authority and the general loss of unity within the body of Christ, especially over the past half-century,have also played a role in this sad development. The proliferation of first hundreds and eventually multiplied thousands of small denominations in the wake of the Civil War Revival led to the general lowering of standards of theological and biblical training for clergy all over the country. Unlike in most of the larger churches, there was no internal demand for proper training. This was quite tragically coupled with a widespread tendency especially within neo-Pentecostalism to mistrust theological schools as anti-Holy Spirit or as caricatured spiritual graveyards.

Once again, hear what Joseph Ali says on this point:

> *The tendency to shy away from the study of theology as a basis for sound Christian doctrine comes as a result of some of the cheap cynical comments some Pentecostal pastors often make of the 'theologians' and 'theology.' We have heard comments like, 'Don't try to bring theology into the word of God; it couldn't work, friends.' Some would say, 'At best, the study of theology gives man only head knowledge that often puffs him up, but messages preached through the power of the Holy Spirit 'a divine utterance from God' is what changes lives.' Others say very proudly, 'We don't teach doctrine (another word for Systematic Theology), we teach only the raw Bible the word of God.' Such negative views and comments about theology and doctrine by some over-zealous gospel preachers seem to suggest that God is against theology and the Holy Spirit has nothing to do with doctrine. For the unstable saints, the obvious conclusion then is to have nothing to do with the commodities God or the Holy Spirit 'abhors.'* [129]

There was some serious truth in the belief that liberal and God-denying theologies had arisen within western churches, starting in Germany and spreading to other western countries. But the reactionary response within segments of the Nigerian Church in rejecting all theological education was disastrous. The result was that pastors and church leaders were progressively unable to serve as adequate guardians of

---

[129]Joseph Mohammed J. Ali, *Op cit*, pp. 22-23.

orthodox Bible teaching. The ensuing seduction of the Nigerian Church by imported false doctrines became virtually inevitable.

Not all of the blame for this failure, however, lies in the hands of church pastors or church leaders. It is regrettable that too often theological schools that have sprung up all over the country have failed to live up to expectations. Many have failed to raise an adequate standard of academic excellence and have tried to carry on with under-trained lecturers, poor facilities, meager textbooks and scarce library resources and in some cases have resorted to offering diplomas and degrees for which they are woefully unqualified. The fact that the errors we have pointed to in this book are often evident even among churches where pastors have formal theological training is a testimony to the inadequacy of the training they have received.

Most of our theological schools have not placed spiritual formation at the top of their agenda and have thereby been unable to turn out men and women on fire for God. Also, very few have developed curricula or mentoring that adequately prepares pastors, evangelists and missionaries for the practical work of the ministry into which they are called. The integration of spiritual gifts with practical ministry is often inadequately handled. In short, Nigeria is in desperate need of better training institutions for the teeming multitude of pastors that the country needs.

If the Nigerian Church is to recover from the sting and death that has been brought on by the seduction we are talking about in this book it will be absolutely imperative to establish much stronger emphases on sound biblical and theological training. There must be a return to a demand for a clergy thoroughly educated in the principles of Bible interpretation, of sound exegesis, and of thoroughgoing biblical theology. All of this can and must be done in a context of spiritual nurturing and formation, where the training of the heart is viewed as equally important with the training of the head.

The truth is that every single error that has seduced the Nigerian Church has not been new teaching but age-old heresies revived and dressed in new and shiny clothes. That our pastors and church leaders have had little or no understanding of the history of theology, and the history of both true and false teachings throughout history has left us vulnerable to shiny objects that were nothing but dressed-up error. Once the shiny objects are embraced and given the seal of approval of more and more church leaders it becomes exceedingly difficult to confront it with the truth.

Yes, we must return to a demand that our pastors pay the price for sound theological training. We are not talking here about merely acquiring certificates either. It is sad that starting in the 1980s Nigeria has witnessed the emergence of literally hundreds of phony Bible schools and theological programs that promise theological degrees of every conceivable description but without criteria that would allow for legitimate outside recognition. In many cases they have teamed up with degree mills from the USA in an attempt to gain legitimacy. Phony Bible schools have proliferated in certain states of the USA where regulations have been weak or nonexistent.

Equally unqualified accrediting associations have also arisen, lending apparent legitimacy to those who do not know better. The result is that today the status of theological education in Nigeria is highly confused and shamefully ill monitored, and solutions do not appear easy. In the meantime the title "Rev.

Dr." in Nigeria has long ago become largely meaningless, along with the title of "Bishop" and even "Archbishop."

Joseph Ali notes on this point:

We in Nigeria seem to be witnessing a warped concept of Christian ministry in recent times, particularly, from the "Full Gospel/Pentecostal/Charismatic" quarters. This distorted view of the Christian ministry is due largely to the lack of sound biblical Christian theology among many preachers. There has always been a tendency to shy away from the study of theology. Even the word "Theology" sounds like a name of some religious demon to some of us. . . . My appeal here is not one born of complaint, however. It is simply that we find means to renew sound biblical and theological training for our churches. I appeal especially to those in our smaller denominations that they find a means of connecting with some of the larger theological schools around the country, which include many that are sound and that remain faithful to Christian orthodoxy.[130]

Consider, by contrast, the description of how one of the most widely renowned proponents of today's Health and Wealth gospel describes his own tutelage: According to his own testimony he took his *"Bible and [Kenneth] Copeland's books for*

---

[130]Joseph Mohammed J. Ali, "The Need for Christian Theology and Sound Doctrine," in *Earnestly Contending*, p. 22. Thankfully, there are a good number of reasonably sound theological schools in Nigeria, though too many for me to name here. In addition to West Africa Theological Seminary (WATS, Lagos), where I have labored for nearly thirty years, I commend great Nigerian seminaries such as the Nigeria Baptist Theological Seminary (NBTS, Ogbomosho), other regional Baptist seminaries and Bible colleges around the country, Jos ECWA Theological Seminary (JETS, Jos), Igbaja Theological Seminary (ITS), Theological College of Northern Nigeria (TCNN, Bukuru), LIFE Theological Seminary (Lagos), Assemblies of God Divinity School of Nigeria (AGDSN, Umuahia), LAWNA Theological Seminary (LATS, Jos), Emmanuel College (Ibadan), Trinity Theological College (TTC, Umuahia), UMCA Theological College (UMTC, Ilorin), Ajayi Crowther Theological Seminary (ACTS, Ogun State), Africa Center for Theological Studies (ACTS, Lagos), Methodist Theological Institute (MTI, Shagamu), etc.

three days and studied them. On the third day light broke through. My prosperity plan is a covenant, not fulfilled until you do your part. I screamed, 'I can never be poor.'" [131]

In a similar vein, Dennis Nweke, writing for the Concerned Ministers Forum, has lamented the tendency among some of pastors to launch into presumed apostolic certainties without adequate preparation.

> *There are a number of pastors who do not have Scriptural spiritual depth, who are often tossed to and fro by every wind of doctrine. When such pastors come in contact with written materials that claim deeper knowledge, their hearts are swayed and, before long, they start preaching heresies. When their supervising authorities try to call them to order, they leave, to start something new, where they will have the liberty to preach all the falsehood they have imbibed.* [132]

RENEWED FOCUS ON SANCTIFICATION

It is easy to lose focus on the central message of the Bible God's never-ending search for fellowship with the people he created in his own image, on the basis of shared character. We have written at some length about the need for holiness in Chapter Six, but we must make a few additional comments here. Fellowship between a holy God and disobedient children is not what God is seeking. That is why God always says, *"You must be holy, because I am holy."* Amos 3:3 asks, rhetorically, *"Can two walk together, unless they are agreed?"* The answer is obvious, and the absolute necessity for the pursuit of holiness therefore can never be denied.

---

[131] David O. Oyedepo, *Understanding the Anointing*, 1998, 2010 reprint, Dominiion Publishing House, p. 109; Oyedepo notes elsewhere of Kenneth Hagin: *"I had read all the books of [Kenneth E. Hagin], until I almost wore out all the pages,"* Oyedepo, *Understanding the Anointing*, 1998, 2010 reprint, Dominion Publishing House, p. 62.
[132] Nweke, Contending, p. 75.

This is the reason we need to have a thorough revival of clear teaching about sanctification and holiness within the Nigerian Church. Words that have fallen out of usage over the past generation must be brought back to our attention with renewed seriousness: consecration, sanctification, brokenness, death to self, the way of the cross, etc. There is nothing magical about these words, of course, but the scriptural theology behind them must be once against strongly embraced.

There is a universal experience among all truly born again believers, and that is that after they have come to God and have tasted the joy of pardon and the thrill of an open relationship with the Lord Jesus sooner or later they discover a deeper need. Sometimes it takes long months riding on high clouds of exuberance in our new life in Christ before we come back to earth enough to discover that lurking deep within our hearts are some very unChristlike characteristics. We are not talking about backsliding into renewed disobedience to God not even in the least. But we begin to discover a double mind within us, with part of us pulling away from the purity of Christ. That is why we may discover things like an ugly spirit of jealousy, and of pride and of carnal anger.

Blessed is the person who when they reach such a point is in a church where there is clear teaching on the need for believers to go on to holiness, and where they can be told exactly what they need to do to surrender to God this time not for pardon but for deeper cleansing and purity. Stirring messages on consecration are important. Such messages can be used of God to show us that though we may have thought we had fully surrendered to Christ when we were born again there is yet a lot of carnal self that is preventing us from deeper consecration. That is when we can more fully understand what Paul meant when he told the Romans, *"knowing this, that our old man was crucified with Him, that the body of sin might be done away with, that we should no longer be slaves of sin"* (Romans 6:6).Even though our "old man" (our former life of constant disobedience and wickedness) had truly been crucified with Christ months earlier, we discover that we are still in many ways a slave to the sin principle with which we were born.

That is also why Paul wrote two chapters later: *"For to be carnally minded is death, but to be spiritually minded is life and peace. Because the carnal mind is enmity against God; for it is not subject to the law of God, nor indeed can be"* (Romans 8:6-7). Where are the churches around Nigeria where believers can hear faithful preaching or discipleship training line-upon-line about how important it is for believers to confront and confess the sinful nature within? Where are the spiritual counselors who can urge such people to take the necessary time to allow the Holy Spirit to show them their spiritual need and to help them discover for themselves what sanctification is all about? Where are our churches where these things are not treated superficially and where earnest seekers after more of God are not told repeatedly,"Tonight, all of your struggles and problems will be over"? Where are our churches where we are told to get serious with God and allow the Holy Spirit to take us step-by-step through a deep consecration and a thorough cleansing?

A. W. Tozer once said that God cannot bless a person greatly until he has hurt him deeply. A central part of Holy Spirit hurting is when he reveals to us the very painful reality of the sin nature yet within our hearts. It is the kind of thing that can leave men and women uncontrollably groaning and crying out to God under agony of soul. Paul echoed some of that in Romans 7:24 - *"O wretched man that I am! Who will deliver me from this body of death?"*

In her most enduring book, *The Christian's Secret of a Happy Life*, Hannah Whitall Smith said this:

> *We must move beyond the shallowness of our crazed and mesmerized subjectivity to be able to say with Job, "Though He slay me yet will I trust in Him," and with David, "Yea, though I walk through the valley of the shadow of death," yet "I will fear no evil; for Thou art with me." Or, "God is our refuge and strength, a very present help in trouble, Therefore, will not we fear, though the earth be removed, and though the mountains be carried into the midst of the sear; though the waters thereof roar and be troubled; though the mountains shake with the swelling thereof. . . . God is in the midst of her; she shall not be moved; God shall help her, and that right early." Or, with Paul, "We are troubled on every side, yet not distressed; we are perplexed, but not in despair; persecuted, but not forsaken; cast down, but not destroyed . . . for which cause we faint not; but though our outward man perish, yet the inward man is renewed day by day. For our light affliction, which is but for a moment, worketh for us a far more exceeding and eternal weight of glory; while we look, not at the things which are seen, but at the things which are not seen; for the things which are seen are temporal; but the things which are not seen are eternal.* [133]

The Concerned Ministers Forum has repeatedly called for a strong focus on holiness and sanctification.

> *What is Holiness? Holiness is a continual separation of life from all sin and for God's use. It begins with initial, critical repentance from sin and continues with spontaneous obedience to any revealed directive from God.* [134]

---

[133] Hannah Whitall Smith, *The Christian's Secret of a Happy Life*, Chapter 18 (Grand Rapids: Fleming H. Revell, 1952).

[134] Mike Oye, *Contending*, p. 40.

Today, the emphasis is on externalism, rituals and legalism. Each denomination seems to have its own code of conduct, not so much based on sound biblical doctrine, but on the 'traditions of the elders.'"[135]

We have the two extremes of legalism and liberalism... Running through the Bible like a golden thread are passages that deal with the subjects of "withdrawal holiness' and 'sacrificial holiness.'...Withdrawal holiness has to do with forsaking every known sin and receiving cleansing in the blood of the Lamb... withdrawal holiness is not a form of monastic life; it is rather a break from sinful habits...Sacrificial holiness is the positive dedication of a sanctified life to God's service. [136]

AFFIRMING OUR PRIMARY MISSION

A final evidence that we have returned to scriptural revival and robust spiritual health will be when the Nigerian Church is once again able to strongly affirm its very reason for existence. This is an exciting prospect that fills our hearts with both hope and determination.

It is clear from Scripture that the Lord Jesus Christ planted the Church for a very specific purpose. Prior to His ascension to heaven He made it clear to His followers that they were to be His witnesses in Jerusalem, Judea, Samaria and unto the uttermost ends of the earth. Yet this witnessing was to be far more than mere verbal proclamation. It was much more fundamentally the testimony of the truth of Jesus' saving power (Hebrews 7:25) through dynamically transformed lives. It is through the transformed lives of Jesus' followers that

---

[135]Mike Oye, *Op cit.*, p. 42.
[136]Oye, pp. 45-46.

God has always intended for the message of the kingdom to be heralded throughout the world.

If there is one thing Satan opposes it is the straightforward message and evidence of moral transformation as God continues to raise up holy, Christlike people in every generation. Our enemy constantly seeks to change the focus of the Church from human sinfulness and the need for moral transformation to a message centered on temporary and materials needs. He has been at it for thousands of years.

However, the mandate that Jesus left the Church has not changed. We still rightfully call it the Great Commission. Evangelism is still our supreme task, and that means drawing as many as possible into deep commitment to Christlike living. The mandate was not simply to proclaim something but to *make disciples*. The primary issue is not how much crowd we are "pulling." Even if we add thousands to our church rolls we will not have genuine success until the Church covers the earth with transformed and holy evangels and exemplars of Christ.

Evangelism is our supreme task. Yet we must regain a clearer picture of what that means. During and shortly after the Civil War Revival the body of Christ that had been made alive was on fire with the burden for personal, usually one-on-one, evangelism. Everywhere they went, and in whatever circumstances, they confronted both friends and strangers alike face-to-face with the claims of the gospel and with a clear call to repentance and Christian discipleship.

By the '80s, however, professionalized mass evangelism began to eclipse personal evangelism. Massive evangelism efforts by Billy Graham, T. L. Osborn and eventually in the 1990s by

Reinhard Bonnke became more and more professionalized and copies by thousands of others. With it, the message imperceptibly changed. From a call to repentance from sin for personal moral transformation, these mass evangelism efforts began to focus gradually more on miracles, signs and wonders, especially as we entered the '90s.

As magnificent as these objectives were, by focusing on material and physical manifestations, they had the regrettable effect of distracting from the spiritual and moral transformation that should have remained the primary objective. Perhaps if there had been more thorough follow-up things could have been different, but it is hard to deny that gradually many of our Nigerian churches became filled with people who had made professions of faith in various campaigns but who did not really understand the central issues of Christian discipleship and of going on to lives of holiness as clearly envisioned and taught by Jesus and the early apostles. This is a major and regrettable part of the story of the Nigerian Church over the past forty years focusing on quantity over quality and in the process submitting to the seductions we have discussed in this book.

Yet we remain convinced that there is great hope. We must begin, first of all, by thoroughly and seriously discipling our current church members. Every one of our church members must realize who they are in Christ. Temptations to mediocrity can be overcome and Satan's ploys to keep God's people from discovering the pathway to sanctification and holiness can be defeated. Death to self-centered living can and must become a reality in our lives.

We must once again become our brothers' keepers by producing manpower within our churches to come alongside those who are coming to the Lord and nurturing them in a deeper walk with God.

The nature of our mass meetings must change moving away from the temptation to highlight signs and wonders and miracles in order to focus more clearly on the eternal battle between sin and righteousness. The call to holiness of heart and life must ring out. Jesus must be seen much more as a spiritual and morally transforming Savior who can pardon sinners and liberate those in moral bondage than as a material and physical miracle worker. We are not saying that miracles are unimportant, but that we should consciously put them in a secondary place behind the need for our people to genuinely repent of their sins and be changed to saints of the Most High.

When this happens we believe the Church can and will gradually rediscover the power of personal evangelism as our primary means of spreading the gospel. Every man's home will at that point become a center from which the gospel will ring forth.

As we engage more and more purposefully in this kind of evangelism it will be apparent that God's ultimate goal for the human race is that we be like Himself. The fall of our original parents into sin meant that their God-like nature was deeply marred. God's essential nature of love was forfeited within the human race. Yet it is now the most ardent desire of the Heavenly Father that His Church be restored to that primal and selfless love. No wonder that Jesus said to His followers, *"A new commandment I give you: Love one another. As I have loved you, so you must love one another"* (John 13:34).

If we see this clearly we will know that any teaching that makes us comfortable with sinful living or with self-centeredness or with greed is a fundamental perversion of the gospel of Jesus

Christ. It is a demonstration of the seduction of Satan. This is why the Church must once again become the arena of love. Sharing together must once again mark the saints of God. The demonstration of care for the needy around us must not be theoretical or merely emotional, but it must become practical. John put it this way:

> *This is how we know what love is: Jesus Christ laid down his life for us. And we ought to lay down our lives for our brothers and sisters. If anyone has material possessions and sees a brother or sister in need but has no pity on them, how can the love of God be in that person? Dear children, let us not love with words or speech but with actions and in truth.* (1 John 3:16-18)

As we write, a large part of the body of Christ in Nigeria has been suffering for many years. The Boko Haram terrorists in the Northeast of the country have repeatedly targeted Christians for killing and destruction. Many belonging to Christ have been reduced to destitution and forced into poorly funded displacement camps. This provides a golden opportunity for those who have not been affected by the mayhem to show our awareness of the oneness of the body of Christ. We can provide regularly towards the needs of these suffering parts of the body. That this is often not the case demonstrates that the body of Christ in Nigeria has been drawn away from the right path through spiritual seduction.

DISCIPLING THE NATIONS

The Great Commission of Jesus Christ relentlessly calls His Church beyond their Jerusalem to the very ends of the earth. The Nigerian Church is not exempted from this call. Our mandate is to make disciples of Jesus Christ in all the nations of the earth. We are not talking about replicating churches that have been emasculated by false teachings and that are focused on self and on material and earthly gain. We have seen far too much of that over the past four decades. We believe we must repent of exporting our seduction to other nations. Rather, we are talking about take the liberating message of life transformation that will lift men and women from the pit of sin and set them on God's highway of holiness and love.

Because the Nigerian Church is one of the largest national churches in the world, it must shoulder a considerable amount of this task. The work of the Nigerian Evangelical Missions Association has already been lauded earlier. More than ever the Nigerian church must rally around her and be more intentional in this great God-given objective. We must raise godly manpower that will go literally to all of the nations of the world with the good news of Jesus Christ. As we have seen, a Church that is primarily concerned with the achievement of material goals will find it difficult or impossible to produce the requisite type of manpower.

As never before, we must learn to "hate" our lives in the here and now so as to find it in the hereafter (Matthew 10:39). We are not talking about the abandonment of everything material or a call to a totally ascetic lifestyle. Rather, we must *prioritize* the hereafter over the material things of this world. As never before we must learn to put the needs of the Kingdom of God ahead of the wants of self.

Over the past decades we have been gradually seduced into self-centeredness. Because of that we have failed to understand that suffering for the sake of the advancement of the Kingdom of God is a great blessing. Yet in coming days we see the potential for a great revival in which the Nigerian Church will arise with strength, will unloose its purse strings, and will become the mighty conquering army that God will use to bring end-time evangelization to a reality around the world.

THE FINAL WORD

It is our firm conviction that the seduction of the Nigerian Church is not inevitably permanent. It can and must be reversed. In this book, we have attempted not only to highlight the causes and indicators of the seduction. We have also tried to show what needs to be done to reverse it.

There are specific signs that we need to look out for that will indicate that the anticipated victory has been achieved. A scripturally reformed and revived Church will return to its primary assignment of effectively making Jesus known by life and words. In doing this, it will abandon emphases on numerical growth through prioritizing public displays of signs, wonders and miracles. It will emphasize the importance of repentance from sin for salvation. It will train, equip and organize its membership for continuous witnessing through their lives, on their jobs, and in their schools, neighborhoods and playgrounds.

To achieve that, the Church will cease feeding members only with messages promoting material prosperity. It will begin to refocus on spiritual transformation unto holiness and sacrificial love among its members. Finally, it will become more intentional in supplying mission efforts and agencies with required manpower, finances and prayers to ensure the effective completion of the Great Commission. When these things begin to once again characterize the Nigerian Church as a whole, we shall celebrate the end of its seduction.

WORKS CITED

Abaya, Mayo; Peter Ozodo, Joseph Mohammed Ali, *Earnestly Contending for the Faith: An Agenda for Responsible Christian Leadership, Second Edition*, (Garki, Abuja: Concerned Ministers' Forum, 1999).

Abodunde, Ayodeji, *A Heritage of Faith: A History of Christianity in Nigeria* (Ibadan: PierceWatershed, 2009).

_________________, *Messenger: Sydney Elton and the Making of Pentecostalism in Nigeria*, (Lagos: PierceWatershed, 2016).

Achebe, Chinua, *There was a Country: A Personal History of Biafra* (New York: The Penguin Press, 2012).

Adeboye, Enoch A., *Come Up Higher With Prayer Points* (Lagos: Printme Communications Company, 2013).

_________________, *Divine Greatness: Classic Expositions from the Holy Ghost*, Oyebanji Oyeyinka andRosamundOyeyinka, eds., (Ibadan: Technopol Publishers, 2012).

_________________, *Doors of Destiny: Classic Expositions from the Holy Ghost*, Oyebanji Oyeyinka andRosamundOyeyinka, eds., (Ibadan: Technopol Publishers, 2012).

_________________, *Fire Power: Classic Prayers and Praises From the Holy Ghost*, Oyebanji Oyeyinka and Rosamund Oyeyinka, eds., (Ibadan: Technopol Publishers, 2012).

_________________, *Reversing the Irreversible: Classic Expositions from the Holy Ghost Divine*, Oyebanji Oyeyinka and Rosamund Oyeyinka, eds., (Ibadan: Technopol Publishers, 2012).

Adeyemo, Tokunboh, *Salvation in African Tradition*. Nairobi: Evangel Publishing House, 1979

Agbenson, Victorson, *Moment of Truth: The Compelling Story of Pastor Tunde Bakare* (Ibadan, Safari Books Ltd, 2014).

Anderson, Allan, "African Initiated Churches of the Spirit and Pneumatology," *Word & World*, Volume 23, Number 2, Spring, 2003.

_________________, *African Reformation: African Initiated Christianity in the 20ᵗʰ Century*, Africa World Press Inc., Trenton, NJ, 2001).

______________, *Moya: The Holy Spirit in an African Context* (Pretoria: University of South Africa Press, 1991).

______________, *Spreading Fires: The Missionary Nature of Early Pentecostalism* (Maryknoll, NY: Orbis Books, 2007.

Aribisala, Femi, "Nigeria's 'Babalawo' Pastors," *Vanguard*, 28 April 2014.

Assemblies of God, "This puts man in the position of using God, rather than man surrendering himself to be used of God." *The Believer and Positive Confession* (Springfield, MO: Gospel Publishing House, 1980).

Bakare, Tunde, "Pastors are Turning to Traders," *Sunday Sun* (Lagos), 25 September 2005.

Barrett, Kurian and Johnson, *World Christian Encyclopedia: A Comparative Survey of Churches and Religions in the Modern World, Second Edition*, (Oxford: Oxford University Press, 2001).

Bounds, E. M., *The Complete Collection of E. M. Bounds on Prayer* (Wilder Publications, 2009).

Brown, Michael L., *Hyper Grace: Exposing the Dangers of the Modern Grace Message*, (Lake Mary, FL: Charisma House, 2014).

Burgess, Richard, *Nigeria's Christian Revolution: The Civil War Revival and its Pentecostal Progeny* (1967-2006) (Eugene, OR: Wipf and Stock, 2008).

Capps, Charles, *How to Have Faith in Your Faith* (Tulsa: Harrison House, 1986).

Christianity Today, "Megachurch pastor stays on despite multiple affairs," July/August 2016, Volume 60, Number 6, pp. 18-19.

Cocks, Tim, "Nigeria's 'megachurches': a hidden pillar of Africa's top economy," Reuters,

October 12, 2014, http://www.reuters.com/article/us-nigeria-megachurches-insight-idUSKCN0I104F20141012. Accessed 12 January 2017.

Copeland, Kenneth, *The Force of Faith* (Fort Worth, TX: Kenneth Copeland Publications, 1983).

______________, "The Force of Love," (Ft Worth: Kenneth Copeland Ministries, 1987), Tape #02-0028.

_______________, *Inner Image of the Covenant* (Fort Worth: Kenneth Copeland Ministries, 1985, audiotape #01-4406), side 2.

_______________, "The Price of It All," *Believer's Voice of Victory*, Sept, 1991, 3-6.

Dayton, Donald W. and Douglas M. Strong, *Rediscovering an Evangelical Heritage: A Tradition and Trajectory of Integrating Piety and Justice* (Grand Rapids: Baker Academic, 2014).

Dilley, Andrea Palpant, "The World the Missionaries Made: The Surprising Discovery About Those Colonialist, Proselytizing Missionaries," *Christianity Today*, January/February 2014, Vol. 58, No. 1, Pg 34.

Farah, Charles Farah, Jr., *From the Pinnacle of the Temple: Faith vs. Presumption* (Plainfield, NJ, 1979).

Fee, Gordon, "The Disease of the Health and Wealth Gospels," (Costa Mesa: Word for Today, 1979).

Ferdinando, Keith, "The Legacy of Byang Kato," International Bulletin of Missionary

Research, Vol. 28, No 4, October 2004, pp. 169-174.

Fuller, Lois, *A Missionary Handbook on African Traditional Religion*, Nigeria Evangelical Missionary Institute, Africa Christian Textbooks, 1st edition, 1994; 2nd edition, 2001).

Gehman, Richard, *African Traditional Religion in the Light of the Bible*, Africa Christian Textbooks, First edition, 2001; 2013).

Grady, J. Lee, "Beware of Doctrines That Tickle Your Ears," *Charisma*, July 2016, p. 70.

The Guardian, November 3, 2016, Vol. 33, No. 13,824, pp, 1, 6.

Hagin, Kenneth E., *How to Write Your Own Ticket with God* (Tulsa, OK: Faith Library, 1979).

_______________, *I Believe in Visions* (Old Tappan, NJ: Fleming H. Revell, 1972).

_______________, *New Thresholds of Faith* (Tulsa, OK: Faith Library Publishers, 2nd ed., 1985 [1972]).

Hiebert, Paul G., "The Flaw of the Excluded Middle," *Missiology: An International Review 10*, (January 1982): 35-47;reprinted in *Anthropological Reflections on Missiological Issues* (Baker Books, 1994), 189-201.

Iorighir, Jonathan, "Gender and The Challenge of Witchcraft," *Living With Dignity: African Perspectives on Gender Equality*, Elna Mouton, Gertrude Kapuma, Len Hansen, Thomas Togom, eds. (Stellenbosch: SUN MeDIA, 2015).

Kalu, Ogbu, *The Embattled Gods: Christianization of Igboland, 1841-1991.*(Lagos: Minaj Publications, 1996).

_________________, "The Third Response: Pentecostalism and the Reconstruction of Christian Experience in Africa, 1970-1995," *Journal of African Christian Thought*, 1:2, 1998.

Kato, Byang, *Theological Pitfalls and Biblical Christianity in Africa*, (Nairobi: Evangelical Publishing House, 1975)

Kenyon, E. W., *What Happened from the Cross to the Throne*, (Lynwood, WA: Kenyon's Gospel Publishing Society, 13th printing, 1969 [1945]).

Kinlaw, Dennis, *Lectures in Old Testament Theology* (Anderson, Indiana: Francis Asbury Press, 2010).

Kowalski, David, "A Brief Overview of the Teachings of Joseph Prince," http://www.apologeticsindex.org/3115-joseph-prince, accessed 10 January 2017.

Kowalski, David, "The Modern 'Grace Message'Revolution or Rebellion?, http://www.apologeticsindex.org/4981-antinomianism, accessed 10January2017.

Lovett, C. S., "The Medicine of Your Mind," *Personal Christianity Newsletter* (Aug 1979).

Luft, Joseph, and Harrington Ingham, "The Johari window, a graphic model of interpersonal awareness," *Proceedings of the western training laboratory in group development* (Los Angeles: University of California, 1955.)

Maduako, D. (et al), *Flame of Fire: The Story of the Scripture Union (Nigeria)* (Ibadan: Scripture Union Press, 2005).

Mbiti, John S., *African Religions and Philosophy* (Heinemann; 2nd Revised

& enlarged edition, 1990).

McCain, Danny, "Addressing Urban Problems Through Kingdom Theology: The 'Apostles in the Market Place' Model in Lagos, Nigeria," in *African Journal of Evangelical Theology*, Nairobi, Volume 32.1, 2013.

_______________, "Final Report of Research Activities and Findings," Nigeria Pentecostal and Charismatic Research Centre (University of Jos, Jos, Plateau State, Nigeria) to Pentecostal and Charismatic Research Initiative, Center for Religion and Civic Culture, University of Southern California, 31 October 2012.

_______________, "From Idahosa to Adeyemi: the Evolving Theology of the Prosperity Gospel in Nigeria" presented at the 42nd Annual Meeting of the Society for Pentecostal Studies, Seattle, Washington on March 22, 2013.

McConnell, D. R., *A Different Gospel, Updated Edition* (Peabody, MA: Hendrickson Publishers, 1988, 1995).

McIntyre, Joe, *E. W. Kenyon and His Message of Faith: The True Story* (Bothell, WA: Empowering Grace Ministries, 1997).

McKnight, Scot McKnight, *Kingdom Conspiracy: Returning to the Radical Mission of the Local Church* (Grand Rapids: Brazos Press, 2016).

Mandryk, Jason, ed., *Operation World, Seventh Edition*, (Colorado Springs: Biblical Publishing, 2010).

Matta, Judith A., *The Born Again Jesus of the Word-Faith Teaching*, (Fullerton, CA: Spirit of Truth Ministry, 1987).

Maxey, Gary S., *Capturing a Lost Vision: Can Nigeria's Greatest Revival Live Again?* (Lagos: WATS publications, 2016).

_______________, *The WATS Journey: A Personal Narrative* (Lagos, WATS Publications, 2014).

Nigeria Evangelical Missions Association (NEMA),

http://nematoday.org/membership/missions.php?gotopage=members Accessed 20 January 2017.

Odesola, Johnson Funso, *Apostle of Holiness: An Expose on E. A. Adeboye's Holiness Concepts* (Lagos: Dynamic ERA Global Services td, 2012).

Ojo, Matthews, *The End-Time Army: Charismatic Movements in Modern Nigeria* (Trenton, NJ: Africa World Press, 2006

Olsen, Ted, "What Really United Pentecostals?" *Christianity Today*, 50:12 (Dec 2006), p. 19.

Onikoyi, Ayo, "How other men of God see TB Joshua," *Vanguard*, September 27, 2014,

http://www.vanguardngr.com/2014/09/men-god-see-tb-joshua/. Accessed 17 January 2017.

Oswalt, John N., *Called to be Holy: A Biblical Perspective* (Anderson, Indiana: Francis Asbury Press, 1999).

Oyedepo, David O., *Anointing for Breakthrough*, 1992, (Lagos: Dominion Publishing House, 1992, 2014 reprint).

_______________, *Exploits in Ministry*, (Lagos: Dominion Press, 2006, reprinted 2013).

_______________, *The Mandate Operational Manual, Living Faith Church Worldwide a.k.a. Winners Chapel International*, (Lagos: Dominion publishing House, 2012).

_______________, *The Miracle Meal* (Lagos: Dominion Publishing House, 2002, reprint 2014).

_______________, *Understanding the Anointing*, (Lagos: Dominion Publishing House, 1998, 2010 reprint).

Phiri, Isaac and Joe Maxwell, "Gospel Riches: Africa's rapid embrace of prosperity Pentecostalism provokes concern and hope," *Christianity Today*, July 2007, Vol. 57, No. 7, p. 23.

Plueddeman, "Missionary Impossible", February 13, 2007, http://missionaryimpossible.blogspot.com.ng/2007/02/byang-kato-biblical- christianity-in.html.

Pollock, John Charles, *The Good Seed: The Story of the Children's Special Service Mission and the Scripture Union* (London: Hodder and Stoughton, 1959).

Prince, Joseph, *Facebook*, June 19, 2013, https://www.facebook.com/josephprince/posts/532289340152253, accessed 18 January 2017.

______________, *Unmerited Favor* (Lake Mary, FL: Charisma House, 2010).

Purkiser, W. T., Richard S. Taylor, Willard H. Taylor, *God, Man& Salvation: A Biblical Theology* (Kansas City: Beacon Hill Press of Kansas City, 1977).

Reasoner, Vic, "Counterfeit Grace," *The Arminian Magazine*, Issue 1-2, Spring & Fall 2015, Vol. 33.

Reeves, Kevin, *The Other Side of the River* (Silverton, OR: Lighthouse Trails, 2007).

Riss, R. M., "Latter Rain Movement," *Dictionary of Pentecostal and Charismatic Movements*, Stanley M. Burgess and Gary B. McGee, eds. (Grand Rapids: Zondervan Publishing House, 1988), pp. 532-534.

Rose, James D., "Leading the Way in Battling Corruption," *Leading an African Renaissance: Opportunities and Challenges*, Springer International Publishing, 2017, pp. 63-74.

Shellnutt, Kate, "Died: Thomas Oden, Methodist Theologian who Found Classical Christianity," *Christianity Today*, December 2016, http://www.christianitytoday.com/gleanings/2016/december.

Smith, Hannah Whitall, *The Christian's Secret of a Happy Life*, Chapter 18 (Grand Rapids: Fleming H. Revell, 1952).

Smith, Timothy L., *Revivalism and Social Reform: American Protestantism on the Eve of the Civil War* (Baltimore: Johns Hopkins University Press, 1980)

Steele, Daniel, *A Substitute for Holiness; or, Antinomianism Revived*, (Eugene, Oregon: WIPF & Stock, 2016), previously published by McDonald, Gill & Co, 1889.

Strang, Steve, "Back from the Brink," *Charisma*, November 2016, Vol. 42, No. 4, pp. 20-24.

Turaki, Yusufu, "The Theological Legacy of the Reverend Doctor Byang Henry Kato," *Africa Journal of Evangelical Theology*, 20:2, 2001, pp. 142-150.

______________, *The Unique Christ: The Challenge of the Non-Christian Religions and Traditional and Modern African Theological Discourse* (Nairobi: International Bible Society, 2001).

Wagner, C. Peter Wagner, *Acts of the Holy Spirit* (Ventura, CA: Regal, 2000).

Weber, Jeremy, "Will Europe's Third-Largest Church Punish Pastor for Multiple Affairs?" Christianity Today, posted 17 May 2016. Accessed 15 June 2016.

Wimber, John, Vineyard '83, Leadership Conference, "The Five Year Plan."

INDEX

In this engaging book, *Capturing a Lost Vision: Can Nigeria's Greatest Revival Live Again?*, Dr. Maxey gives first-hand accounts of Nigeria's Civil War Revival in the 1960s and 1970s. He examines the DNA of the revival and the reasons for its decline. More importantly, he poses the vital question of whether Nigeria can once again see a revival of equal or greater impact.

"This book will re-ignite hunger for revival in the heart of the reader. . . . Dr. Maxey shares exciting perspectives to the Nigerian Civil War revival that are worth reading by all pastors, students of history and scholars. After going through this book, one must agree that there has been a dramatic shift in the Church and that there is a compelling need to return to our lost heritage. Let us humbly invite God to heal his Church." (Pastor Austen Ukachi, He's Alive Chapel, Lagos)

"As a partaker of the 70s revival, my heart was filled with emotion as I read the truth detailed in this book. Hot tears welled up in my eyes. Then a voice said to me, 'Don't cry. Greater things are ahead.' May we live to see it!" (Dr. Uzodinma Obed, Apostolic Discipleship Movement, Ibadan)

Order your copy today:

Outside Nigeria: amazon.com (ebook on Kindle).

In Nigeria:

Marketing and Distribution enquiries to:
WATS Publications
West Africa Theological Seminary, 36, Olukunle Akinola Street Akinyele/WATS Bus Stop, Ipaja Ayobo Road, Lagos, Nigeria.
www.watspublications.com, sales@watspublications.com
Tel: +234 (0) 803 781 2817; +234 (0) 806 875 2197; + 234 (0) 802 312 2408 To order copies, please contact: sales@watspublications.com

Or: ACTS bookshop and other Christian book outlets near you.

You can also order via: amazon.com (Kindle or hard copy), konga.com or watspublications.com

Recounts the exciting journey of Gary and Emma Lou Maxey and their four children from the time of their arrival in Nigeria in March 1982 to the 25th anniversary of West Africa Theological Seminary, in 2014.

"This is a fascinating book, a breath-taking account of the inspired adventure of an American family who ventured into Nigeria in 1982 with the sole aim of founding a Theological College that would address the crying need of training African Church Pastors. . . ." Rev. Prof. E. M. Uka, Prelate, Presbyterian Church of Nigeria.

"I have known Gary and Emma for the past 20 years and I am impressed, as many others, with the great work and contribution they have made in the training of Christian leadership for the Church in Nigeria and Africa. . . ." General Dr. Yakubu Gowon, GCFR (President of Nigeria, 1966-1975).

"Throughout the book I smiled, laughed, cried, rejoiced, sometimes mourned. and found myself praying, 'Do it again, God!'" - Dr. William Sillings, Chairman, Friends of WATS

Order your copy today:

Outside Nigeria: amazon.com (ebook on Kindle).

In Nigeria:
Marketing and Distribution enquiries to:
WATS Publications
West Africa Theological Seminary, 36, Olukunle Akinola Street Akinyele/WATS Bus Stop, Ipaja Ayobo Road, Lagos, Nigeria.
www.watspublications.com sales@watspublications.com
Tel: +234 (0) 803 781 2817; +234 (0) 806 875 2197; + 234 (0) 802 312 2408 To order copies, please contact: sales@watspublications.com Or: ACTS bookshop and other Christian book outlets near you. You can also order via: amazon.com (Kindle or hard copy), konga.com or watspublications.com

The first book in the twelve-volume discipleship series entitled *Teach Me Your Paths*. This is superior discipleship material for Sunday schools, small groups or individual Christian growth. It is a strong starting point for anyone who seriously wishes to learn the ways of our God. You cannot understand Bible doctrine correctly without obeying God and entering into personal relationship with the Lord (John 7:17; 1 Corinthians 2:14). Therefore, experiencing one's own new life in Christ should be the beginning of proper study of Christian doctrine.

In this book, Part One (Lessons 1-8) tells about the New Birth, the wonderful experience in which a condemned and powerless sinner is made a new creature in Christ. Part Two (Lessons 9-16) tells about Sanctification, involving both crisis and process, beginning at the New Birth and continuing on throughout the life of the believer. Sanctification includes purifying of the heart and progressive transformation into the image of Christ, and it is the right and necessity of every born-again believer. Part Three (Lessons 17-24) tells about some of the issues involved in Christian growth in grace, the need of every child of God, ensuring that we persevere to the end of our race here on earth.

Subsequent volumes in this series take believers through the entire spectrum of Christian biblical and theological education to provide comprehensive discipleship training for the Church.

Order your copy today:

Outside Nigeria: amazon.com (ebook on Kindle).

In Nigeria: Marketing and Distribution enquiries to:

WATS Publications West Africa Theological Seminary, 36, Olukunle Akinola Street, Akinyele/WATS Bus Stop, Ipaja Ayobo Road, Lagos, Nigeria. www.watspublications.com, sales@watspublications.com
Tel: +234 (0) 803 781 2817; +234 (0) 806 875 2197; + 234 (0) 802 312 2408. To order copies, please contact: sales@watspublications.com Or: ACTS bookshop and other Christian book outlets near you.

You can also order via: amazon.com (Kindle or hard copy), konga.com or watspublications.com

This book was originally published more than thirty years ago by Rev. I. Parker Maxey, father of Dr. Gary S. Maxey. It was reprinted several times in its original American format and widely used in Nigerian Bible colleges over the past twenty years. Now this revised and Africa-contextualized edition has been produced to continue to fill a large gap in material for pastoral training for Nigeria.

Dr. Gary S. Maxey has overseen the editing of this African edition, particularly relying on the expertise of three African pastors and trainers of pastors who had opportunities to study under the original author during his numerous visits to Nigeria in the 1990s. Dr. William Udotong (who served at WATS for over twenty years, including seven years as provost), Dr. Acha Goris (who is married to one of I. Parker Maxey's granddaughters), and Rev. John Onwuka (long-time pastor of pastors) have teamed up to make this book the best on the market for ministerial ethics and etiquette.

A Guide to Ministerial Ethics & Etiquette already has a proven track record in Nigeria. We are convinced that this new edition will go much further yet.

Order your copy today:

Outside Nigeria: amazon.com (ebook on Kindle).

In Nigeria: Marketing and Distribution enquiries to:
WATS Publications, West Africa Theological Seminary, 36, Olukunle Akinola Street, Akinyele/WATS Bus Stop, Ipaja Ayobo Road, Lagos, Nigeria. www.watspublications.com,
Tel: +234 (0) 803 781 2817; +234 (0) 806 875 2197; + 234 (0) 802 312 2408 To order copies, please contact:
sales@watspublications.com Or: ACTS bookshop and other Christian book outlets near you.

You can also order via: amazon.com (Kindle or hard copy), konga.com or watspublications.com

Discovering the Old Testament is the second title in the series, Teach Me Your Paths. The first title, New Life in Christ, has been well received, and the expectation is that the ten books that are to follow will provide a robust library for introducing the basics of Christianity especially to pastors, Sunday school teachers, small group leaders and others seeking to understand our Christian faith better.

This second book is a journey through the first part of the Bible, the Old Testament. It starts with an overview of the Bible and some general issues before plunging into the thirty-nine books that make up the Old Testament. It is a well-known fact that the Old Testament is of keen interest to Africans. In many senses they find themselves more at home with the largely rural cultures of the Old Testament than do some other cultures around the world. A grasp of the history and content of God's word as revealed in the Old Testament is very fundamental to our foundation in God's revelation. We believe the present and future strength of the African Church will be far greater if we can hold this revelation very close to our hearts.

Order your copy today:

Outside Nigeria: amazon.com (ebook on Kindle).

In Nigeria:

Marketing and Distribution enquiries to:
WATS Publications
West Africa Theological Seminary, 36, Olukunle Akinola Street Akinyele/WATS Bus Stop, Ipaja Ayobo Road, Lagos, Nigeria.
www.watspublications.com Tel: +234 (0) 803 781 2817; +234 (0) 806 875 2197; + 234 (0) 802 312 2408. To order copies, please contact: sales@watspublications.com Or: ACTS bookshop and other Christian book outlets near you. You can also order via: amazon.com (Kindle or hard copy), konga.com or watspublications.com

Confessions of a Grateful Pilgrim: Reflections @ 70, is the spiritual autobiography of Dr. Gary S. Maxey. In an unusually candid summary of his spiritual odyssey, he takes us all the way from his misunderstanding and rejection of God in his early childhood to his present activities as a pastor, seminary founder and writer. Confessions are certainly there, but also many reasons why he is today a grateful pilgrim with high hope for heavenly rewards.

Dr. Maxey describes how he came into a dynamic walk with God at age seventeen, including his personal discovery of the meaning of holiness. He also tells candidly recounts his lengthy battle with the return of pornographic addiction that had marked his childhood, and how it was eventually overcome. With similar candor he tells how after nearly thirty years of peaceful and productive marriage he faced a storm of marital stress and failure that lasted for several years before it was happily resolved.

This is a story of hope for anyone facing the common struggles of living out the Christian life in the modern world.

Order your copy today:

Outside Nigeria: amazon.com (ebook on Kindle).

In Nigeria:
Marketing and Distribution enquiries to:
WATS Publications
West Africa Theological Seminary, 36, Olukunle Akinola Street
Akinyele/WATS Bus Stop, Ipaja Ayobo Road, Lagos, Nigeria.
www.watspublications.com Tel: +234 (0) 803 781 2817; +234 (0) 806 875 2197; 1 234 (0) 802 312 2408. To order copies, please contact: sales@watspublications.com Or: ACTS bookshop and other Christian book outlets near you. You can also order via: amazon.com (Kindle or hard copy), konga.com or watspublications.com

The two-fold objective of this book is to show a clear picture of what a holy woman or man should look like and to describe the pathway for its attainment. *The Highway of Holiness* is metaphorical for the life of holiness that starts at the point of the New Birth and progresses throughout our lifetimes. Scripturally, all believers are saints, or holy ones, yet there is also discernible progress along the way. The author uses 2 Thessalonians 2:13, which describes our salvation to be  "through the sanctification of the Holy Spirit" to talk about the operations of the Holy Spirit in illumination, separation, purification and inhabitation. In doing so, he builds on several decades of ministry in Nigeria both as a teacher and pastor.

Order your copy today:

Outside Nigeria: amazon.com (ebook on Kindle).

In Nigeria:
Marketing and Distribution enquiries to:
WATS Publications
West Africa Theological Seminary, 36, Olukunle Akinola Street Akinyele/WATS Bus Stop, Ipaja Ayobo Road, Lagos, Nigeria. www.watspublications.com Tel: +234 (0) 803 781 2817; +234 (0) 806 875 2197; + 234 (0) 802 312 2408. To order copies, please contact: sales@watspublications.com Or: ACTS bookshop and other Christian book outlets near you. You can also order via: amazon.com (Kindle or hard copy), konga.com or watspublications.com